THE ULTIMATE
BOOK OF
NUMBER PUZZLES

**Including
Number Puzzles
More Number Puzzles
A Third Book of Number Puzzles
Magic Square Puzzles**

D1324962

THE ULTIMATE BOOK OF NUMBER PUZZLES

KENNETH KELSEY
and
DAVID KING

CRESSET

This omnibus edition first published in 1992 by
Cresset

incorporating

Number Puzzles
First published in Great Britain 1979 with the title *The Cunning
Caliph* by Frederick Muller Ltd
© K. J. Kelsey 1979

More Number Puzzles
First published in Great Britain 1981 by Frederick Muller Ltd
© K. J. Kelsey 1981

A Third Book of Number Puzzles
First published in Great Britain 1984 by Frederick Muller Ltd
© K. J. Kelsey 1984

Magic Square Puzzles
First published in Great Britain in 1984 by Frederick Muller Ltd
© David King 1984

Printed and bound in Great Britain

0 09 177204 4

NUMBER PUZZLES

Contents

Introduction

A few years ago I had occasion to call upon one of the Directors of the Rijksgebouwendienst in The Hague. On the wall of his office was a carved stone plaque, retrieved from a derelict seventeenth century Dutch farm house. It consisted of the following square:

16	3	2	13
5	10	11	8
9	6	7	12
4	15	14	1

and underneath was the word 'Compatibility'.

The Director explained that the square's compatibility arose from the fact that the figures 1 to 16 were so arranged within the square, that the horizontal, vertical and diagonal lines all added up to 34.

It was my first introduction to a magic square, a fact I now find surprising since magic squares have been around for two or three

1

thousand years, and the plaque I saw was not original but a replica of the wall plaque depicted in Albrecht Durer's engraving 'Melencolia I', dating from 1514, and now in the British Museum.

The square intrigued me from the start. Its compatibility was not limited to the horizontal, vertical and diagonal lines. The following groupings also added up to 34:

the four quarters,
the centre four squares,
the four corners,
the centre squares, top and bottom,
the centre squares, left and right, and
the two pairs of squares across diagonally opposing corners.

Since that day in The Hague, the pursuit of magic squares has become a hobby, not limited to the four power square shown above but encompassing also five, six, seven, eight and higher-order squares. Their unique characteristics lend themselves admirably to puzzles, since, by applying logic and elementary arithmetic, the puzzler can build up and complete any given magic square with the aid of just a few clues.

This book is a collection of some of the puzzles I have devised for the amusement of my family and friends. I hope you enjoy them too.

1

The Resourceful Wife

The solicitor was reading the eccentric's will.

"To my faithful gardener, Jack," he read, "I bequeath the sum of £1,000, with the request that part of the money be spent in planting a rose-garden with 50 rosebushes within each of five circles, and 50 rosebushes in each of ten rows, no two beds containing the same number of bushes."

"At £1 a bush," said Jack, "I reckon I'll only have £250 left of that legacy."

"At £1 a bush," said Jack's wife, "I reckon you can hang on to £800."

"How?" said Jack.

"Easy," said his wife. She drew the sketch below and began filling in the number of rosebushes to be planted in each bed.

"I get it," said Jack. "Don't fill in any more. I can work the rest out myself."

Can you?

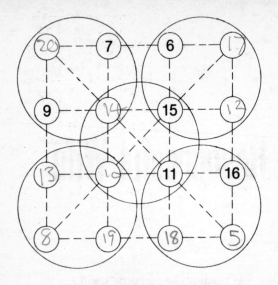

This is a basic puzzle, making use of the characteristics of a four power square, that not only do the horizontal, vertical and diagonal lines add up to the same number, but so also do the four quarters and the centre four squares. A magic square comprised of the figures 1 to 16 has a constant of 34. The puzzle above is based upon a constant of 50, that is 16 greater than a basic square. Since there are four squares to each line, it follows that the increment per square is 4, and the range of figures used is 5 to 20 inclusive.

The next four puzzles follow the same pattern, and can be solved by the application of further characteristics, namely that the centre squares, top and bottom; the centre squares, left and right; and the two pairs of squares across diagonally opposing corners, also add up to the same constant.

Complete the magic squares below to produce constants of 34, 46, 54 and 62 respectively.

Puzzle No. 2

	3		14
8			12
11		6	

Puzzle No. 3

8		14	
	19		5
11			
		9	

Puzzle No. 4

	21		
12		11	
19			
	10	14	

Puzzle No. 5

20			23
		16	
		14	
10	22		

2

The Cunning Caliph

A Caliph, renowned for his cunning, once said to his tailor, "You say I owe you more, yet I say I owe you but 34 gold pieces. Since we cannot agree, and I am a generous man, I will allow you to make a greater profit, if Allah so wills. Here are 16 boxes, arranged in four rows of four. See, I am placing 1 gold coin in this box, 2 in this box, 3 in this box, and so on to 16 in this last box. You can see where all the gold coins lie. You may choose any four boxes in a row, be it horizontal, vertical or diagonal."

The tailor studied the boxes and after a while said, "Sire, it matters not which row I choose, for they all contain 34 gold pieces."

"My generosity is boundless," said the Caliph. "You may choose any four boxes which themselves form a square."

The tailor studied the boxes again, then said, "Sire, all such squares contain exactly 34 gold coins."

"I am just, as well as generous," said the Caliph. "Before you choose, you may move any number of rows from the left side to the right, or from the top to the bottom, or do both."

The tailor studied the boxes yet again. "Sire," he said at last, "Your generosity I question not, yet not matter how I move the boxes, I cannot change the number of gold coins in any such grouping of four. Truly has Allah shown me that you owe me but 34 pieces of gold."

In what order had the cunning Caliph placed the coins in the boxes? The contents of five boxes are shown.

1			
		3	
			2
14			11

This puzzles makes use of the special characteristics of the pan-diagonal magic square, that is, one which retains its magical qualities even when one or more rows is transposed from the top to the bottom, or from the left to the right, or both. Further characteristics of such a pan-diagonal square are: (a) not only the four quarters and the centre four squares add up to the constant, but so also do any four squares which together form a square, and (b) any corner square plus the three squares across the diagonally opposing corner also add up to the constant.

For these reasons it is possible to solve pan-diagonal puzzles with fewer clues than are required with puzzles based upon basic squares.

Complete the pan-diagonal magic squares below to produce constants of 38, 42, 50 and 58 respectively.

Puzzle No. 7

5			
	17		7
	12	9	

Puzzle No. 8

		14	
	17		
			18
	16	9	

Puzzle No. 9

17		20	
5			
		9	14

Puzzle No. 10

13			
18			12
	17		10

3

The Kyrosian Tactic

The commander of the Kyrosian forces is planning to attack neighbouring Zukar with a fleet of 16 space-ships arranged in orbit around Zukar, as shown in the diagram below. Each space-ship carries a different number of cosmic rocket launchers, ranging from 5 in the smallest craft, 6 in the next, and so on through to 20 in the largest, making a total of 200 rocket launchers in all. The Kyrosian commander knows that the Zukarians have perfected a disintegrating ray device which will eliminate four of his ships, and which could be brought to bear upon his fleet in any one of three ways, namely, against any four space-ships along the same radius; against any four space ships in the same orbit; or against any four space-ships in the same spiral. The commander knows that the Zukarians can use this weapon only once, and although he knows that he will lose four space-ships, he has so arranged his fleet that whichever way the disintegrating ray is brought to bear, he will still be left with 150 of his 200 rocket launchers.

How did he position his fleet?

The position of six of his space-ships is given.

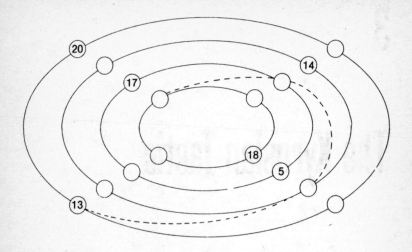

'Planetarium' puzzles such as this can be formed only from pan-diagonal magic squares, since the eight spirals, four in each direction, correspond to the eight diagonals and broken diagonals of a pan-diagonal square.

The radial lines correspond to the horizontal lines of the square, and the orbital lines correspond to the vertical. With this information it should be possible to solve planetarium puzzles with as few clues as were needed to solve the pan-diagonal puzzles in Chapter 2, but there is something about the visual presentation which many find inhibiting. The following four puzzles will test your ability to overcome the visual 'blockage', if such there be.

Complete the following planetarium puzzles to produce constants of 34, 50, 62 and 70 respectively.

Puzzle No. 12

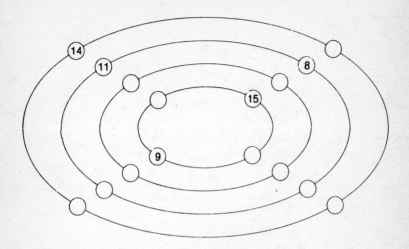

Puzzle No. 13

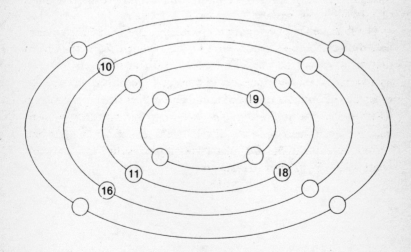

11

Puzzle No. 14

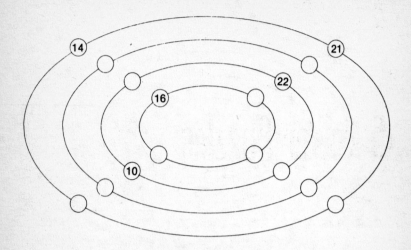

Puzzle No. 15

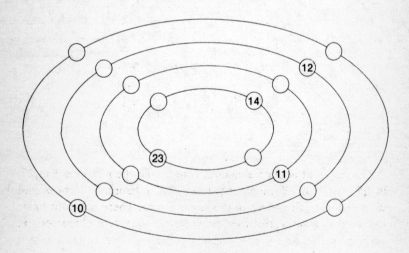

4

5 Power Puzzles

The following is a typical basic 5 power magic square:

17	24	1	8	15
23	5	7	14	16
4	6	13	20	22
10	12	19	21	3
11	18	25	2	9

The constant of such a square, comprising the numbers 1 to 25, is 65. As with all magic squares, the horizontal, vertical and diagonal lines all add up to the same figure. There are both basic and pan-diagonal varieties of the 5 power square. A characteristic of both is that any symmetrical grouping of five squares which includes the centre square, for example the four corners and the centre square, also produces the constant. A further characteristic of the basic square, but not the pan-diagonal square, is that each pair of diametrically opposed numbers add up to the sum of the highest and lowest figures in the square (in the example above, 26), and the centre square is always occupied by the mean figure (in the example above, 13).

The following five puzzles are all based upon the basic 5 power square:

Complete the five magic squares below to produce constants of 65, 70, 75, 80 and 85 respectively.

Puzzle No. 16

2	15			8
10				
14			4	
		9		

Puzzle No. 17

		26		3
	19			20
18			6	
	5			21

Puzzle No. 18

		7		9
10				18
	14	3		
				17

Puzzle No. 19

	21	10		
9			26	15
	8			
	27			

Puzzle No. 20

	28	18		14
	21			9
				24
	12			

5

The War Game

At the NATO Headquarters on the outskirts of Brussels a War Game was in progress. The Allied officers on the course had been split into groups and occupied several small Operations Rooms, each of which was equipped with visual display panels and computer consols. In one such room the officers who had been designated White Force K were studying the orders which had just appeared on their display panel. It read:

You are to attempt to secure a beach-head in Sector 7. You will attempt the landing with a force of 500 Commandos deployed in 25 landing craft, each craft carrying a different number of personnel. The landing craft will approach the beach in a five-by-five box formation.

The Umpires will notify Red Force M defending the Sector of the exact deployment of your men among the craft.

Five of your landing craft will be destroyed before reaching the beach. Red Force M will nominate the five by choosing five craft in any horizontal, vertical or diagonal line, or any five adjacent craft which together form a cross.

To simulate an error in communication, the Umpires may re-arrange your box formation by moving any number of lines from the left flank to the right, or from the front to the rear, or they may do both.

If you suffer more than 20% troop losses you will be deemed not to have secured the beach-head.

You have 30 minutes to notify the Umpires of your troop deployment.

Timed: 12.03.

After a minute or two, one of the officers said, "Surely our losses will be a matter of pure chance?"

"I'm not so sure," said another. "I can't believe that these War Games are just a sophisticated form of gambling. No, there's a solution here somewhere. Clearly we can't reduce the number of men in any one grouping without increasing it in another, thus making that group more vulnerable. We must assume that Red M will make no errors of judgment, so we must work out a deployment which will place 100 men in every horizontal, vertical and diagonal line, and in every cross formation, despite any re-arrangement which the Umpires may make."

He was right, of course. At 12.30 White K relayed their troop deployment to the Umpires, and at 12.58 their display panel read:

"Beach-head secured. Losses: 100 men and five craft."

How had they deployed the Commandos? The number of men in eight of the landing craft is given below.

	9			
	27		19	
29				
	13		30	
25				14

The War Game puzzle utilizes the special characteristics of a pan-diagonal 5 power square, namely that any number of rows can be transposed from the left side to the right, or from the top to the bottom, or both, without destroying the square's magical qualities. Since the rows and columns can be so moved, it follows that the centre square can be occupied by any figure, and not just the mean. A further characteristic is that any five adjacent squares in cross formation (× or +) will also produce the constant.

For these reasons the pan-diagonal puzzles can be solved with fewer clues than were necessary to solve the basic puzzles in Chapter 4. In those puzzles the complementary numbers to each of the clues are immediately ascertainable. This is not the case with pan-diagonal 5 power puzzles.

Four further examples of such pan-diagonal puzzles follow.

Complete the magic squares below to produce constants of 65, 70, 80 and 90 respectively.

Puzzle No. 22

2		15		
	24		7	
				4
	5		13	
	18			10

Puzzle No. 23

	25		18	
		12		10
			4	
5		23	7	

Puzzle No. 24

		26		
			9	
4		23		
			6	13
16			22	

Puzzle No. 25

	6		29	
19				7
				28
	18		12	
				16

6

The Zukarian Counter

The Zukarians have long feared an attack from neighbouring Kyros and have determined upon a pre-emptive strike. To this end they have stationed a fleet of 25 space-ships in orbit around Kyros, as shown in the diagram below. Each space-ship carries a different number of cosmic rocket launchers, ranging from 8 in the smallest craft, 9 in the next, and so on through to 32 in the largest, making a total of 500 rocket launchers in all. They fear, however, that the Kyrosians may also possess a disintegrating ray device which could eliminate 5 of their space-ships, and which could be brought to bear upon their fleet in any one of three ways, namely, against any five space-ships along the same radius; against any five space-ships in the same orbit; or against any five space-ships in the same spiral. They have therefore arranged their fleet so that whichever way the disintegrating ray is brought to bear, they will lose only 100 of their 500 rocket launchers.

How have they positioned their fleet?

The position of eleven of their space-ships is given.

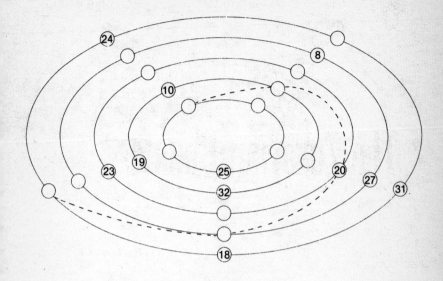

As might be expected, the pan-diagonal 5 power magic square lends itself to the 'planetarium' form, and, just as with the 4 power planetarium puzzles, it should be possible to solve such puzzles with as few clues and as easily as the puzzles in the previous chapter. But is it?

The following four puzzles should tell.

Complete the following four planetarium puzzles to produce constants of 70, 80, 90 and 100 respectively.

Puzzle No. 27

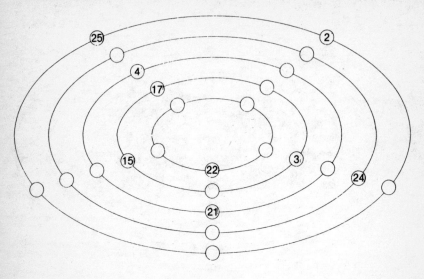

Puzzle No. 28

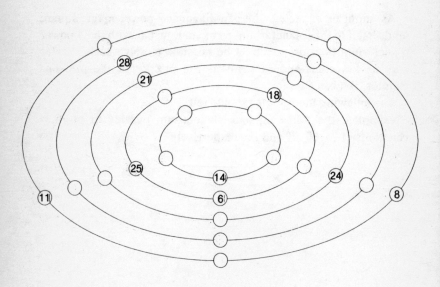

Puzzle No. 29

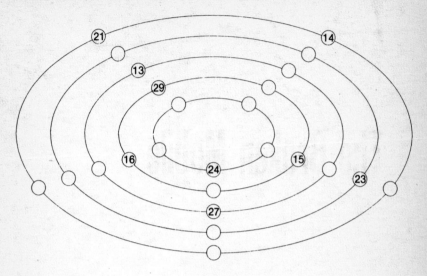

Puzzle No. 30

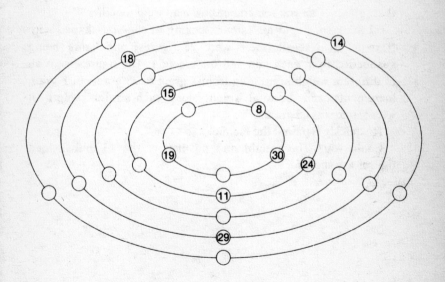

23

7

The Broken Mobile

"Daddy," said David, "I have had a slight mishap with the mobile you made for me, and only 13 of the figures have remained in their places. Can you remember how it all went together?"

"I think so," said his father, looking at the star-shaped wire frame. "As I recall, there were 25 figures, one figure being suspended from each join and intersection. The figures were all of different weights, ranging from 1 gram to 25 grams in 1 gram increments, and the total weight along each straight length of wire frame was 65 grams."

He quickly repaired the mobile.

Could you? The weight and position of the 13 undislodged figures are shown.

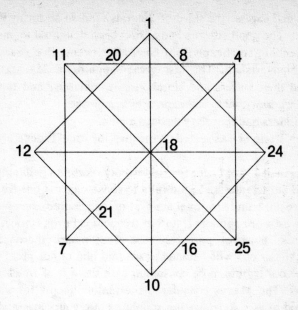

All 5 power pan-diagonal magic squares can be set out in this star form. After I had set this particular puzzle and given it to some friends to solve, a lively exchange took place as to whether such a mobile would be in balance. It was suggested that I had failed to learn what I had been taught at school about turning forces and moments. Eventually we decided to construct one with exactly the same weight distribution and position. Whether our workmanship was faulty or there was an inherent error in my hypothetical mobile I do not know, but there was a distinct tilt towards the corner supporting the 25 grams. So, for the avoidance of doubt, I re-wrote the puzzle as . . . . . .

The Star of T'ang Li

T'ang Li, the War Lord, was visiting the city of Liang Chang to receive his annual tribute. Twenty-five years earlier he had granted the citizens their freedom against a yearly payment of one pure sapphire. The first sapphire was to be of 1 carat, the second of 2 carats, the third of 3 carats, and so on for as long as he lived. The good citizens had at first been delighted to purchase their freedom so cheaply, but now, after twenty-five years, they were impoverished. The last great sapphire of 25 carats had emptied their coffers and storehouses completely, and they had not the wherewithal to make the tribute now due.

The Elders had therefore devised a plan.

When T'ang Li was seated on the dias, the Chief Elder addressed him thus:

"Excellent T'ang Li, for five and twenty years now, willingly have we paid out tribute, and gratefully have we enjoyed our freedom. Yet were our tribute to equal our gratitude in degree, then would it need to be more abundant, for our freedom is beyond price, while sapphires, however pure, are not. Last month there came a Magus to our city who listened as we told him of our great desire to make our tribute more consonant with the gift of freedom you gave us. The Magus considered the matter deeply for a while, then said to us, 'Retrieve the sapphires into your care, and have them set as a star for T'ang Li's turban. Set the great sapphire of 25 carats in the centre and arrange the others about it in the mystical order which I shall reveal to you, so that in each direction, along every line, the weight of the sapphires is exactly 65 carats. With this rich star in sublime equilibrium set upon his head, T'ang Li will enjoy for all time the approbation of the Gods. No greater tribute than this can you pay him. And just as true freedom can be granted but once, so a perfect tribute requires no reiteration.'"

In such a fashion did the wily Elders quit themselves of their burden.

How did they arrange the sapphires?

The position and weight of twelve of the stones is given.

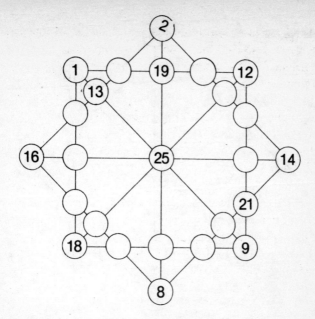

Three similar puzzles follow, all requiring completion to produce a constant of 65.

Puzzle No. 33

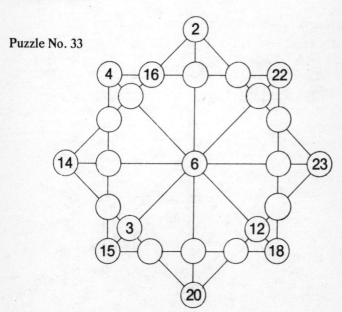

Puzzle No. 34

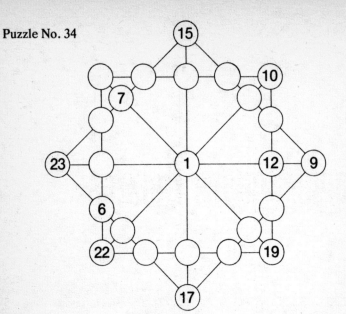

Puzzle No. 35

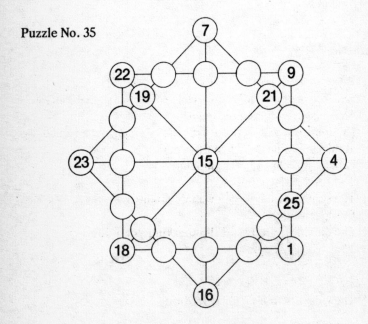

8

Magic Square Quizzes

The answers to the following quizzes are the numbers 1 to 25. When they are correctly positioned with the help of the clues given, the horizontal, vertical and diagonal lines will all add up to 65.

1. Little bird under par.
2. Party leader's dream house.
3. Decennoval.
4. She was married, charming, chaste and . . . . . . (Byron)
5. Shakespeare night at the theatre.
6. Dr. Johnson sadly reflected that he knew almost as much at this age as he did when fifty-four.
7. Haydn's 'Philosopher' Symphony.
8. The sixth prime number.
9. The singer would like a few more minutes.
10. European figure. .
11. The distance, professionally speaking, for a title.
12. They were just men.
13. Endless figure.
14. $\sqrt{289}$.
15. The Queen's first birthday in April.

16. Irritation after so many years.
17. 12^2
18. Lady Day.
19. The result of pounding a stone.
20. Sheets, in the wind . . . . .
21. . . . . . and in a quire.
22. As it's the baker's, it's bigger!
23. How many hours should a dog watch?
24. "Why, sometimes," said the Queen, "I've believed as many as . . . . . impossible things before breakfast."
25. Icosahedral.

Puzzle No. 36

1	2	3	4	5
6	7	8	9	10
11	12	13	14	15
16	17	18	19	20
21	22	23	24	25

1. Louis executed in 1793.
2. Martinmas.
3. Lovely February day.
4. An impossible score in cribbage.
5. Take a piece of Brubeck.
6. "Then it ought to be number . . . . ." said Alice.
7. $17 + 19$.

8. "That's a strong breeze," said Admiral Beaufort.
9. and 10.   The date President Monroe expounded his doctrine.
11. Letters in the Greek alphabet.
12. These yards belong to a chain.
13. One third of the Church's Articles.
14. A pair of braces.
15. An eagle.
16. Little Maids who, all unwary.
     Come from a ladies' seminary. (The Mikado)
17. They are often blue, being in the same boat.
18. The year the Mayflower sailed in the 17th Century.
19. The number of elms between the bridges at Chelsea and Wandsworth.
20. April day for our antipodean comrades.
21. What guinea-pigs used to cost?
22. Sisters who stay on the coast outside Eastbourne.
23. It's glorious in August, especially on the moors.
24. Yo-ho-ho, and a bottle of rum!
25. Pins, American style.

Puzzle No. 37

1	2	3	4	5
6	7	8	9	10
11	12	13	14	15
16	17	18	19	20
21	22	23	24	25

1. and 2. "Sent to hear sermons
From mystical Germans
Who preach from . . . . . till . . . . ." (The Mikado)
3. England's saintly day in April,
4. and Ireland's in March.
5. The Chancellor's town house.
6. and 7. Napoleon's retreat from Moscow.
8. Catherine Parr was Henry's.
9. A certain number of beans.
10. A day in October for the U.N.
11. Fine day or night of love.
12. 9^2
13. The club house is such a hole.
14. Guests at the Last Supper.
15. Dopey & Co.
16. "L'Etat c'est moi," he said.
17. The maximum number of bells on board.
18. Marriage leaves them still . . . . . fools. (Congreve)
19. 15×25.
20. The thousands of Cornishmen who will know the reason why.
21. A road to Eastbourne.
22. Sex to decimalise? Partly!
23. Let's hope it doesn't rain this July.
24. Possession means so much.
25. Sightless rodents.

Puzzle No. 38

1	2	3	4	5
6	7	8	9	10
11	12	13	14	15
16	17	18	19	20
21	22	23	24	25

1. A third of the way up Buchan's steps.
2. A pounds worth of ounces.
3. Icositetrahedral.
4. When we . . . . . parted in silence and tears. (Byron)
5. Were there not . . . . . cleansed? (St. Luke)
6. The half hour sounded ten minutes ago.
7. Which number Watling Street?
8. $\sqrt{4^3}$
9. He's a bit undersized and you don't feel surprised.
   When he tells you he's only . . . . . (Iolanthe)
10. A Metonic cycle takes such a long time.
11. According to Dr. Johnson, Shakespeare never wrote more
    than . . . . . lines together without a mistake.
12. 14 — 9.
13. Tennyson's Maud is not.
14. Half the United States are.
15. Man's unusual number of legs, or are they arms?
16. Quires in a ream.
17. The tenth prime number.
18. Mahler's 'Titan' Symphony.
19. Ennead.
20. Substitute man.
21. Mediaeval poster.
22. Such deadly sins.
23. Beware this March day.
24. There are several holes, of course.
25. Card game, not bridge, but could be.

Puzzle No. 39

1	2	3	4	5
6	7	8	9	10
11	12	13	14	15
16	17	18	19	20
21	22	23	24	25

1. A sporty number on the side.
2. Catchy little number, isn't it?
3. Not the end of the world, but world war I.
4. Days of wonder.
5. Beethoven's 'Emperor' Concerto.
6. Figure or pieces.
7. Square.
8. Pride of Lions.
9. Mozart's Piano Concerto, the theme music for Elvira Madigan.
10. Inside it's even teenier.
11. Silver Anniversary.
12. 7^2
13. Kings of Essex.
14. A crowd.
15. July day for the French.
16. Company.
17. The original number of States in the Union.
18. Pied blackbirds.
19. Quite a score.
20. Beethoven's 'Pastoral' Symphony.
21. The record for teenagers.
22. Gallons of hats.
23. Catherine of Aragon was Henry's.
24. A panel of jurors.
25. The Lord is my Shepherd.

Puzzle No. 40

1	2	3	4	5
6	7	8	9	10
11	12	13	14	15
16	17	18	19	20
21	22	23	24	25

9

5 Power Number Jigs

The following five puzzles are equivalent to jig-saw puzzles, the repeated numbers providing the clues as to where the sequences of numbers interlock. For the first four puzzles you have to arrange the sequences of numbers, some horizontally and some vertically, within the adjacent grid in such a way that all the horizontal, vertical and diagonal lines add up to 65. The fifth puzzle is slightly harder, in that the sequences can also be inserted in the grid diagonally.

6, 14, 17, 5.
17, 8, 4, 15.
10, 19, 23.
22, 18, 9.
11, 8, 25.
12, 1, 10.
21, 3, 20.
2, 13, 24.
12, 9, 21.
16, 7, 3.

			24	
		22		
23				

Puzzle No. 41

4, 10, 17, 14.
12, 9, 16, 22.
6, 19, 21.
23, 2, 7.
5, 25, 13.
4, 15, 21.
24, 3, 8.
18, 1, 24.
20, 7, 5.
5, 11, 22

	10			
			8	
6				

25, 4, 8, 12.
15, 19, 23, 2.
22, 9, 16.
6, 24, 12.
15, 3, 16.
18, 5, 12.
22, 1, 10.
7, 11, 20.
13, 17, 21.
14, 21, 8.

				18
		17		
16				

4, 16, 8, 25.
6, 23, 15, 2.
24, 5, 6.
16, 22, 3.
14, 20, 21.
12, 18, 24.
17, 11, 10.
3, 9, 15.
19, 13, 7.
25, 1, 7.

12				
	11			
			13	

36

16, 25, 4, 8.
14, 7, 5, 23.
10, 3, 21, 19
9, 22, 15.
13, 24, 10.
13, 2, 16.
25, 18, 11.
6, 17, 3.
15, 8, 1.
6, 4, 22.
20, 1, 12.

16				
			17	
	18		15	

10

6 Power Number Jigs

The next five puzzles are based upon the six power magic square. Such squares comprised of the numbers 1 to 36 have a constant of 111. They are not as versatile as other magic squares, as they have no pan-diagonal version. The following puzzles follow the same pattern as the 5 power number jigs. For the first four you have to arrange the sequence of numbers, some horizontally and some vertically, within the adjacent grid in such a way that all the horizontal, vertical and diagonal lines add up to 111. The fifth puzzle is slightly more difficult, as the sequence of numbers can also be inserted in the grid diagonally.

12, 3, 21, 26, 34.
6, 18, 13, 31, 20.
7, 35, 8, 32.
14, 20, 28, 25.
23, 17, 30, 12.
36, 4, 6, 35.
29, 5, 2.
15, 9, 14.
24, 19, 33.
1, 31, 33.
22, 27, 11.
16, 10, 25.

Puzzle No. 46

3					
				2	
	4				
				1	

20, 5, 26, 13, 32.
30, 12, 23, 7, 21.
4, 17, 22, 33.
11, 35, 20, 18.
15, 21, 31, 14.
25, 28, 19, 16.
4, 8, 5.
34, 27, 1.
24, 6, 15.
10, 29, 31.
2, 36, 3.
7, 29, 9.

Puzzle No. 47

	8				
			13		
18					
		3			

6, 15, 22, 31, 18.
19, 34, 14, 16, 3.
34, 1, 33, 32.
31, 2, 27, 7.
16, 30, 20, 17.
13, 24, 8, 12.
32, 11, 17.
14, 10, 26.
9, 23, 21.
25, 29, 13.
5, 36, 28.
3, 35, 4.

Puzzle No. 48

		15			
	10				
		20			
			5		

9, 8, 32, 31, 30.
16, 27, 20, 17, 10.
34, 18, 19, 3.
26, 21, 7, 12.
2, 13, 24, 35.
22, 1, 11, 16.
15, 30, 26.
16, 36, 25.
8, 32, 31.
5, 28, 7.
1, 9, 8.
36, 6, 29.

Puzzle No. 49

				6	2
	8				
		4			

29, 26, 23, 8, 11.
4, 13, 12, 33, 24.
16, 19, 1, 14.
24, 5, 21, 15.
17, 22, 35, 11.
36, 6, 34, 28.
25, 36, 16.
2, 27, 18.
9, 31, 35.
10, 20, 21.
30, 15, 18.
5, 27, 7.
1, 32, 3.

Puzzle No. 50

	6				
	10				
				7	
			9		
				8	

11

The Incomplete Print-Out

The nuclear research station superintendent was briefing his computer manager.

"This is a sketch plan of a packing box in which we have to store 9 rods of fissile material. The circular holes, arranged in three rows of three, are to house the rods, and the 16 square compartments surrounding them are to house the graphite packing. The 9 rods have weights ranging from 46 ounces through to 54 ounces, by 1 ounce increments. Because of their critical mass, they have to be stored in such a way that the weight of any row, either horizontally, vertically or diagonally, does not exceed 150 ounces."

"You don't need a computer to solve that problem," said the computer manager.

"I know," said the superintendent, "but that is only half the story. For the fissile material to remain stable indefinitely, the graphite packing, which ranges from 30 ounces through to 45 ounces, also by increments of 1 ounce, must itself be so arranged that the weight in any row, either horizontally, vertically or diagonally, and the weight in each of the four quarters and in the centre four compartments, is exactly 150 ounces in all cases."

Returning with the computer print-out a little later, the manager said, "I'm afraid the computer broke down halfway through the print-out, and only a few of the figures have been printed. However, I'm sure there's sufficient information here for your chaps to derive the rest."

He was right. The incomplete computer print-out is shown. Can you complete it?

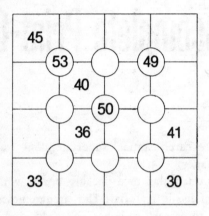

This puzzle demonstrates the fact that any magic square can be set into any other magic square of one higher power, both magic squares having the same constant. The 3 in 4 power combination is the only one that is practical for puzzle purposes, with a constant of 150. Other combinations become increasingly cumbersome. For example, a 4 in 5 power square would have a constant of 410, and a 5 in 6 power square would have a constant of 915. There are many variations of the 3 in 4 power square, four of which follow. You are required to complete the squares so as to produce a constant of 150 in every case.

Puzzle No. 52

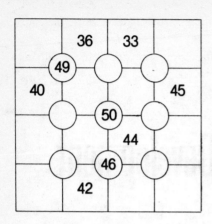

Puzzle No. 53

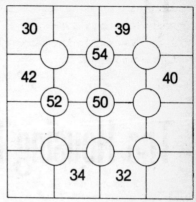

Puzzle No. 54

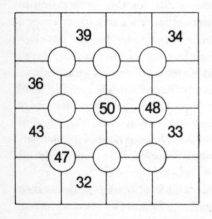

Puzzle No. 55

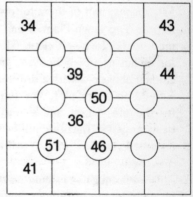

12

The Housing Development

The Local Authority has set aside a site for the construction of 528 houses, half of them for owner occupation and half for council letting. The Town Planner has been asked to lay out the development in 32 plots — sixteen (shown as circles in the sketch below) for owner-occupied houses, and sixteen (shown as squares) for council houses — with a different number of houses, ranging from 1 to 32 on every plot. For the purposes of providing uniformity for the gas, water and electricity connections, the plots are to be arranged so that the number of both council houses and owner-occupied houses in any direction, horizontally, vertically or diagonally, is 66.

The Planner has calculated the number of houses to be erected on 12 of the plots. Can you complete the lay-out?

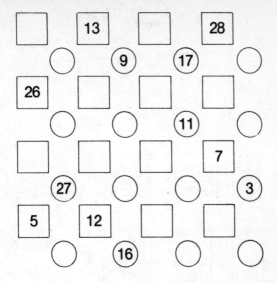

Just as one can arrange the numbers 1 to 16 to form one magic square with a constant of 34, so one can arrange the numbers 1 to 32 to form two magic squares with a constant of 66 (as in the puzzle above); the numbers 1 to 48 to form three magic squares with a constant of 98; and the numbers 1 to 64 to form four magic squares with a constant of 130. When one positions the last four to form a square, one has an 8 power magic square with a constant of 260!

Try to work through the sequence with the aid of the clues in the grids below. All the squares are pan-diagonal, so if you remember the ground rules set out in Chapter 2 you should have no difficulty. The single square has a constant of 34; the pair of squares each have a constant of 66; the trio of squares each have a constant of 98; and the final four squares each have a constant of 130.

Puzzle No. 57

8			
3		9	16
	12		

Puzzle No. 58

	12		
20			
		28	
	24	13	

		18	
19			6
		23	
		14	

Puzzle No. 59

	19	25	
24		13	
	42		

	26		
14			32
	44		23

	34		4
27			
		28	15

<table>
</table>

		40	
48		9	
25			8

5		29	
			12
	53	4	

50		2	
7			
	23	58	

		38	
	14		3
	62	11	

Puzzle No. 60

As was mentioned earlier, when these last four squares are positioned together as one large square, they form an 8 power magic square with a constant of 260. Since the four smaller squares are pan-diagonal, an 8 power square will be formed even if you transpose any of the rows of any of the squares, or turn any of them through 90°, 180°, or 270°, or do any combination of those things! The 8 power square will not itself be pan-diagonal, however.

13

The Knight Errant

"My liege," said the young knight, "set me a task, I pray you, that I might find honour, fame and fortune in your service."

The King therefore led him to a square courtyard paved as is a chequer-board, with tiles of black and white, sixty-four in number. The yard was bare, but in one corner stood a cell with door both barred and bolted.

The King pointed. "Sir Knight," he said, "know you that two years back my youngest daughter was imprisoned in yon cell, cast there under a spell by wicked Bandar. None can lift the spell and draw the bolts save any knight who, entering upon the courtyard here, and moving only as a chess knight moves, smites with his sword every tile in turn, the first tile once, the second twice, the third thrice and thus unto the sixty-fourth tile outside the cell. The sum of the number of smites in every row, both North to South and East to West, must equal 260, and the sum mid-way in each direction must equal half that sum. Then, and only then, will the spell be lifted and the bolts be drawn. Lift the spell, and you shall have my daughter's hand in marriage, with honour, fame and fortune enough. Fail, and you will surely perish under Bandar's spell, as have the many brave knights who have gone before."

The young knight drew his sword, and stepping into the court-yard, smartly smote the first tile once . . . . .

No royal hand in marriage awaits you if you succeed in tracing the young knight's steps to the cell door, but then, neither will you surely perish if you don't. To help you though, the fourth of all his moves is given.

		49				17	64
1				33			
	29		45		61		13
		53		37			
			5		21		
		25		9			
			41		57		

I have been unable to work out more than four variations of this interesting knight's move square — ignoring rotations and reflections. It is not a true magic square, since the diagonals do not produce the constant, and cannot do so since the diagonals of the main square, and of the four smaller squares which comprise it, are either wholly even or wholly odd, an impossibility for a 4 power square.

Three more such puzzles follow, two with the third of each move being given, and one with the fourth.

1		31			16		
		46			19		
		49			34		64
52		4			61		13
43			28	37			22
7		25			40		58
	55					10	

		49			34		64
		46			19		
1		31			16		
52		4			61		13
		25			40		
28							37
43		55			10		22
			7	58			

1				33			
		49				17	64
	29		45		61		13
5		25		9		21	
	53		41		57		37

14

Topsy-Turvy

Below is a magic square with a constant of 264. Turn it upside-down, and the constant is still 264!

By introducing the figure '0', compile a 5 power magic square which also has a constant of 264 whichever way up it is.

16	88	69	91
99	61	86	18
81	19	98	66
68	96	11	89

Puzzle No. 65

96			0I	
		99		
		0		91
	98			
				68

15

Magic Cubes

All 4 power magic squares can be extrapolated to form a magic cube, that is to say, a cube with each of its six planes displaying a different magic square, and with all contiguous bordering squares having the same value as the squares they touch.

See example on following page:

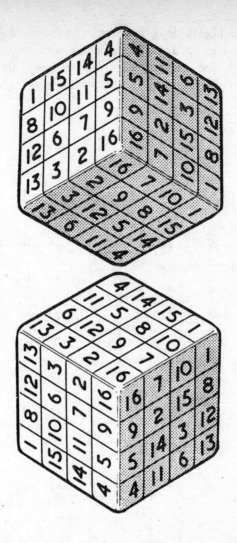

Given one completed plane of a magic cube, therefore, one has four clues for each of four other planes. We have seen earlier that, given six clues (five for pan-diagonals) one can build up the original plane of a magic cube. It needs very few additional clues to complete it.

The diagram below depicts a cube in its two-dimensional form. From the clues given, and with the additional knowledge that the uppermost square and the third square down are both pan-diagonal, complete the cube. The constant is 34.

Puzzle No. 66

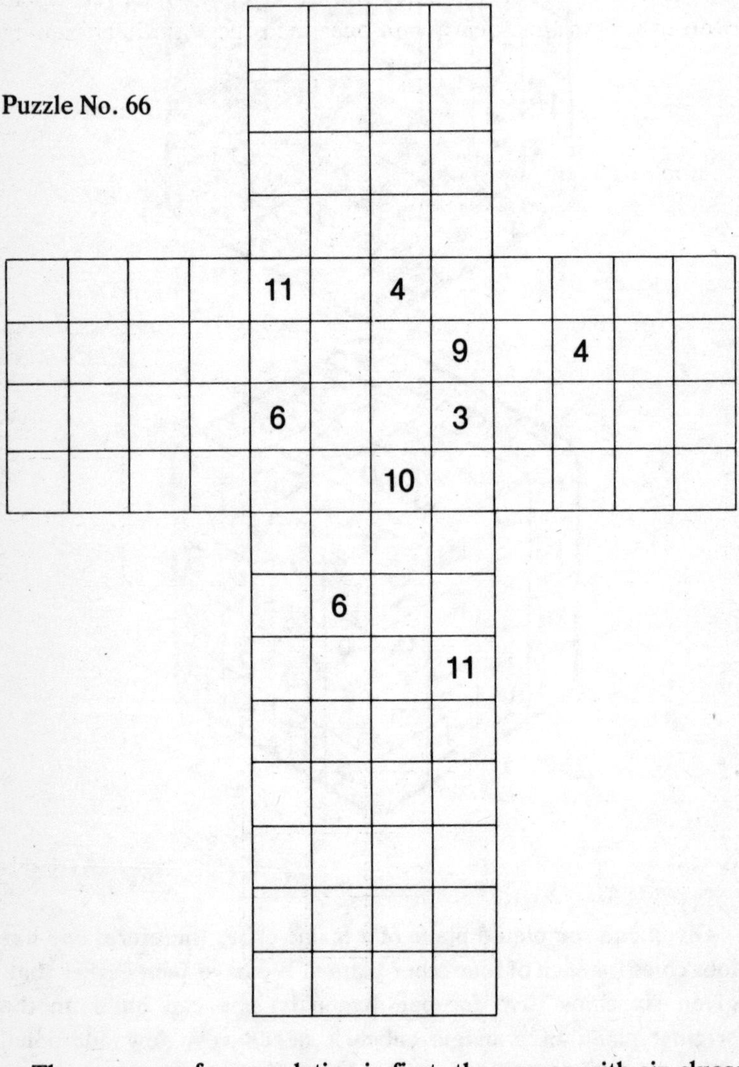

			11		4				
					9		4		
			6		3				
				10					

	6		
		11	

The sequence for completion is first, the square with six clues;

56

then the square with two; then the square with one; then the uppermost square. The other two are then simple.

In this next example the left hand and right hand squares are pan-diagonal. Complete the cube to produce a constant of 34. The sequence is first the square with six clues; then the square with two, then the square with one; then the right hand square.

Puzzle No. 67

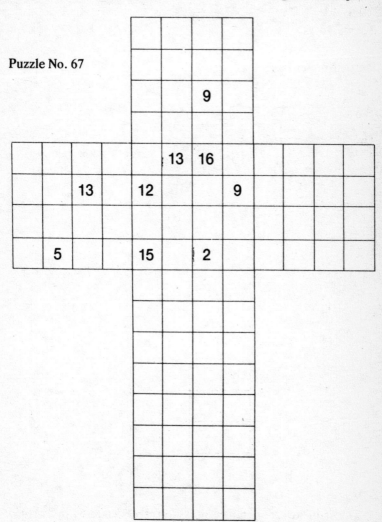

In the next example the second square down and the bottom square are both pan-diagonal. The constant is still 34, and the sequence should now be apparent.

Puzzle No. 68

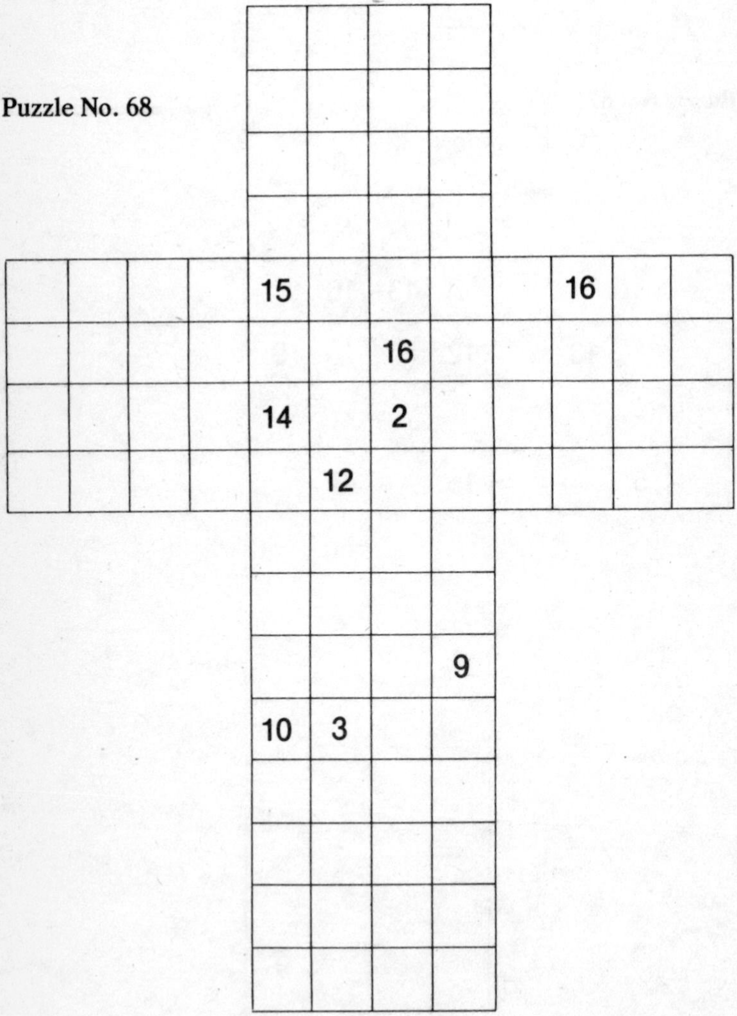

			15			16					
				16							
			14	2							
			12								
					9						
			10	3							

58

In this next example there are no pan-diagonal squares, and consequently more clues are given. The sequence is first, the square with six clues; then the square with three; then the third square down; then the bottom square; then the left hand square. The final square is simple. The constant is 34.

Puzzle No. 69

				14		7		9			
				4			16				
											4
					10	6		12			
					7						
				16							

59

In this final example, the pan-diagonal squares are the uppermost square and the third square down, as in the first example given. The sequence is the same, and the constant is 34.

Puzzle No. 70

16

Magic Crystals

Magic squares are basically cross-sums, with a marked degree of 'compatibility', as the Dutch wall plaque pointed out. This degree of compatibility makes it possible to express the 4 power square in a variety of ways, such as the following 'crystal' shape. Using all the numbers 1 to 16, number the corners in the following diagrams so that the corners of each of the seven rectangles contained in the diagrams add up to 34. In each case eight numbers are provided as clues.

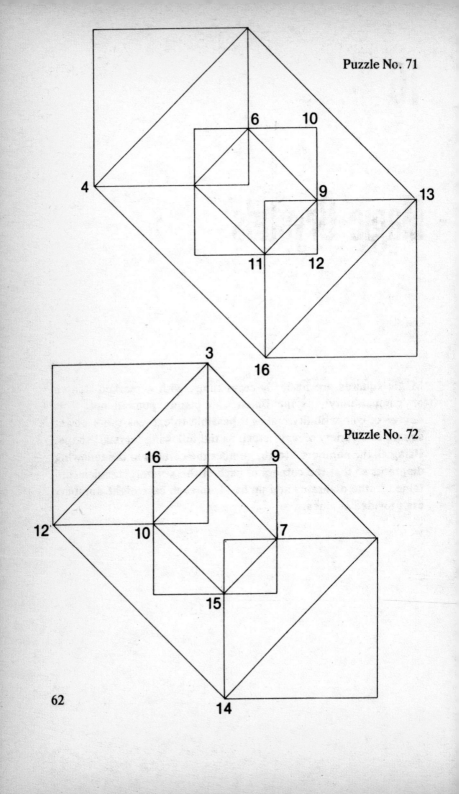

Puzzle No. 71

Puzzle No. 72

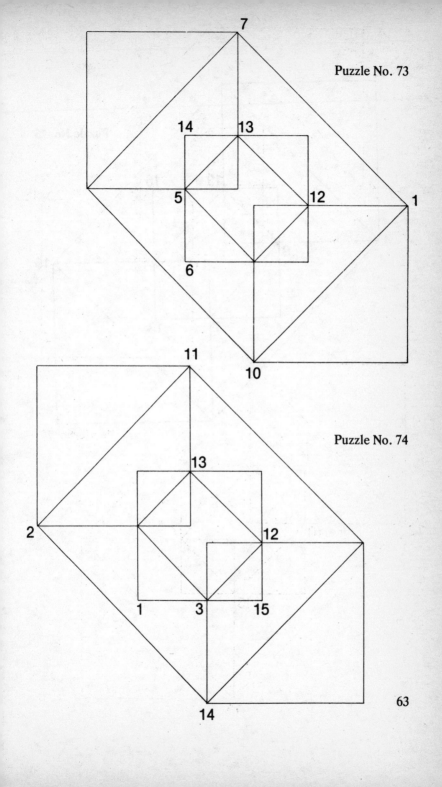

Puzzle No. 73

Puzzle No. 74

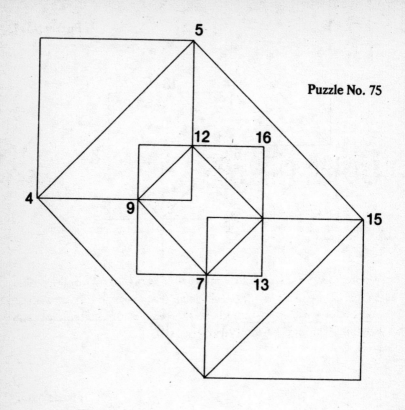

5

12   16

4

9

15

7   13

17

Other Shapes

Magic squares also lend themselves to cross-sums forming other shapes. Here are a few. In each case the sum of the numbers along each line is 34, even though in the case of the six-pointed star not all the numbers from 1 to 16 are used.

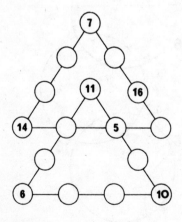

Puzzle No. 76

Puzzle No. 77

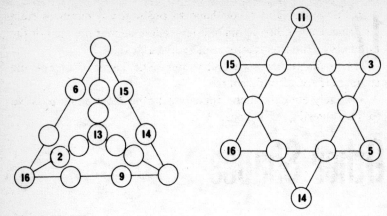

Puzzle No. 78

Puzzle No. 79

Puzzle No. 80

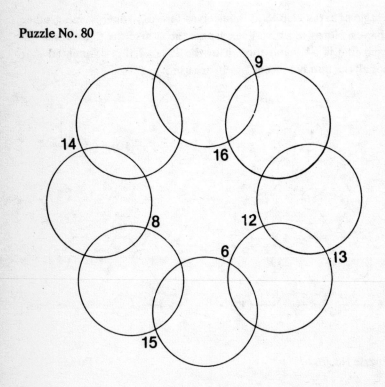

In the puzzle above you have to position the numbers from 1 to 16 at each of the points of intersection, so that the sum of the numbers on the circumference of every circle is 34.

Try to find other such cross-sums. The logos of automobile companies are a fruitful source.

Strangely enough, there appear to be no cross-sums possible for the following two shapes.

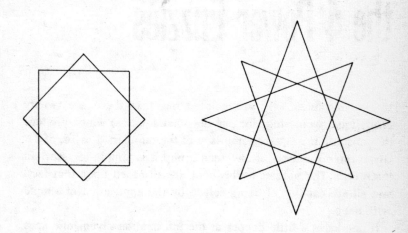

18

Hints on solving the 4 Power Puzzles

In the Introduction it was pointed out that there are twenty groupings (twenty-four for pan-diagonal squares) which produce the constant, in a square comprised of the numbers 1 to 16, of 34. Given three numbers of any such group it is simple to ascertain the fourth. The puzzles in this book are all based upon that fact, and all are capable of being solved by the application of simple arithmetic.

If one looks a little deeper at the information given, one sees that it is possible to derive further data to make the solving of the puzzles even easier. For example, in the diagram of a 4 power square below, the squares marked with an 'A' total 34, as do those marked with a 'B'.

AB	AB	A	A
B	B		

Two of the squares, those marked 'AB', are common to both equations, so it follows that the two remaining 'A' squares equal the two remaining 'B' squares. Given three of those four numbers, therefore, it is possible to derive the fourth.

Applying the same logic to all possible situations, we can ascertain that there are 24 groupings (28 for pan-diagonal squares) for which, given three of the numbers, it is possible to derive the fourth. These groupings are set out in the six diagrams below. As the magic square is symmetrical, the pattern of the six examples is repeated to produce the 24 (or 28) possible situations.

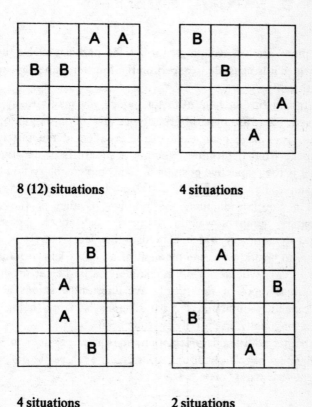

8 (12) situations   4 situations

4 situations   2 situations

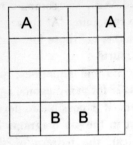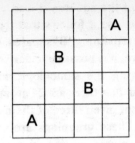

4 situations

So there are 44 groupings (or 52 for pan-diagonal squares) from which it is possible to ascertain the fourth number, given the other three.

There is a further helpful factor, which you may already have observed. There are nine different types of 4 power magic square, and all types have been used in the creation of the puzzles in this book. What determines whether a square is of one type or another is the respective position of the complementary numbers, for example, 1 and 16, 2 and 15 and so on. In the very first example given in the Introduction, the relative position of the complementary numbers was in diametric and equal opposition. Given two numbers which establish this fact, therefore, it is possible to position the complement of all other known numbers in the square, whether or not it completes a particular grouping. The various types of square all have different positions for the complementary numbers, the pan-diagonal square's being next but one diagonally, in the only possible position.

With this additional information, it is now possible to solve pan-diagonal puzzles with only four clues, such as the following which has a constant of 34,

Puzzle No. 81

	3		
5			4
	2		

or perhaps you would prefer to work out the two possible solutions to another pan-diagonal puzzle with only three clues, but still with a constant of 34.

Puzzle no. 82

			8
	6		
14			

Solutions

20	7	6	17
9	14	15	12
13	10	11	16
8	19	18	5

The Resourceful Wife

2	3	15	14
13	16	4	1
8	5	9	12
11	10	6	7

No. 2

8	7	14	17
12	19	10	5
11	4	13	18
15	16	9	6

No. 3

6	21	9	18
12	15	11	16
19	8	20	7
17	10	14	13

No. 4

20	8	11	23
15	19	16	12
17	13	14	18
10	22	21	9

No. 5

1	15	10	8
12	6	3	13
7	9	16	2
14	4	5	11

The Cunning Caliph

5	6	11	16
10	17	4	7
8	3	14	13
15	12	9	2

No. 7

10	3	14	15
12	17	8	5
7	6	11	18
13	16	9	4

No. 8

17	6	20	7
16	11	13	10
5	18	8	19
12	15	9	14

No. 9

13	8	22	15
18	19	9	12
7	14	16	21
20	17	11	10

No. 10

The Kyrosian Tactic

No. 12

No. 13

73

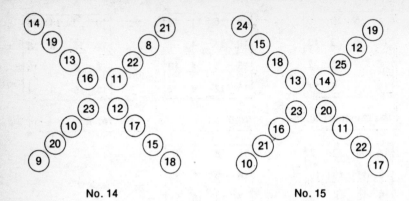

No. 14

No. 15

2	15	17	23	8
10	22	1	20	12
21	19	13	7	5
14	6	25	4	16
18	3	9	11	24

No. 16

7	11	26	23	3
12	19	4	15	20
18	22	14	6	10
8	13	24	9	16
25	5	2	17	21

No. 17

13	24	7	22	9
10	4	27	16	18
19	25	15	5	11
12	14	3	26	20
21	8	23	6	17

No. 18

19	21	10	5	25
9	18	12	26	15
28	8	16	24	4
17	6	20	14	23
7	27	22	11	13

No. 19

23	5	8	22	27
10	28	18	15	14
25	21	17	13	9
20	19	16	6	24
7	12	26	29	11

No. 20

18	9	15	26	32
16	27	28	19	10
29	20	11	17	23
12	13	24	30	21
25	31	22	8	14

The War Game

2	6	15	19	23
20	24	3	7	11
8	12	16	25	4
21	5	9	13	17
14	18	22	1	10

No. 22

8	17	6	15	24
16	25	9	18	2
19	3	12	26	10
22	11	20	4	13
5	14	23	7	21

No. 23

12	19	26	18	5
28	15	7	9	21
4	11	23	25	17
20	27	14	6	13
16	8	10	22	24

No. 24

23	6	17	29	15
19	30	13	21	7
11	22	9	20	28
10	18	26	12	24
27	14	25	8	16

No. 25

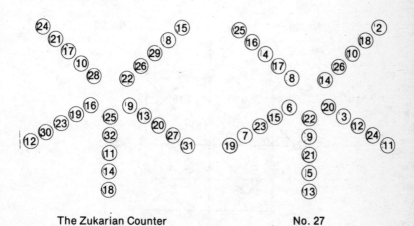

The Zukarian Counter

No. 27

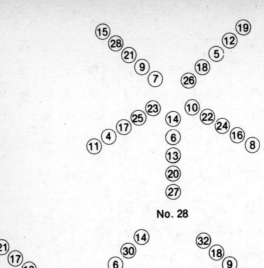

No. 28

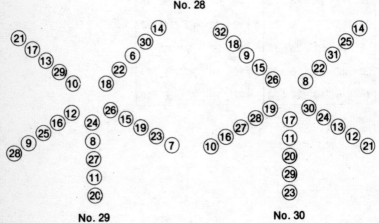

No. 29

No. 30

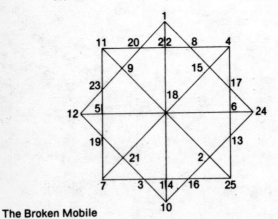

The Broken Mobile

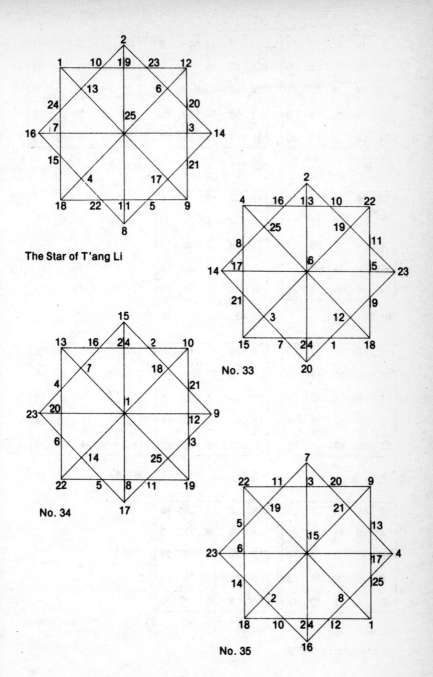

The Star of T'ang Li

No. 33

No. 34

No. 35

77

1	10	19	23	12
18	22	11	5	9
15	4	8	17	21
7	16	25	14	3
24	13	2	6	20

No. 36

16	11	14	19	5
1	17	6	18	23
24	22	13	4	2
3	8	20	9	25
21	7	12	15	10

No. 37

10	4	23	17	11
18	12	6	5	24
1	25	19	13	7
14	8	2	21	20
22	16	15	9	3

No. 38

13	16	24	2	10
22	5	8	11	19
6	14	17	25	3
20	23	1	9	12
4	7	15	18	21

No. 39

11	22	18	9	5
8	4	15	21	17
25	16	7	3	14
2	13	24	20	6
19	10	1	12	23

No. 40

6	2	13	24	20
14	25	16	7	3
17	8	4	15	21
5	11	22	18	9
23	19	10	1	12

No. 41

4	10	17	14	20
15	18	23	2	7
21	1	13	25	5
19	24	3	8	11
6	12	9	16	22

No. 42

22	1	10	14	18
9	13	17	21	5
16	25	4	8	12
3	7	11	20	24
15	19	23	2	6

No. 43

12	18	24	5	6
4	10	11	17	23
16	22	3	9	15
8	14	20	21	2
25	1	7	13	19

No. 44

16	2	13	24	10
14	25	6	17	3
7	18	4	15	21
5	11	22	8	19
23	9	20	1	12

No. 45

12	3	21	26	34	15
30	36	29	5	2	9
17	4	24	19	33	14
23	6	18	13	31	20
7	35	8	32	1	28
22	27	11	16	10	25

No. 46

11	4	17	22	33	24
35	8	34	27	1	6
20	5	26	13	32	15
18	30	12	23	7	21
2	36	3	10	29	31
25	28	19	16	9	14

No. 47

19	6	15	22	31	18
34	1	33	32	2	9
14	10	26	11	27	23
16	30	20	17	7	21
3	35	4	5	36	28
25	29	13	24	8	12

No. 48

22	1	11	16	36	25
34	9	33	27	6	2
18	8	23	20	29	13
19	32	14	17	5	24
3	31	4	10	28	35
15	30	26	21	7	12

No. 49

25	4	13	12	33	24
36	6	34	28	5	2
16	10	20	21	27	17
19	30	15	18	7	22
1	32	3	9	31	35
14	29	26	23	8	11

No. 50

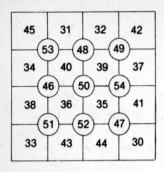

The Incomplete Print-Out

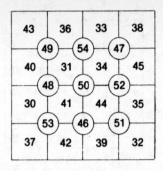

No. 52

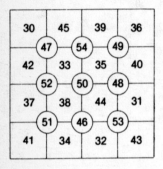

No. 53

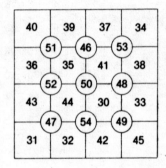

No. 54

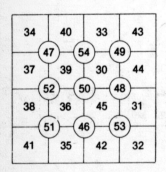

No. 55

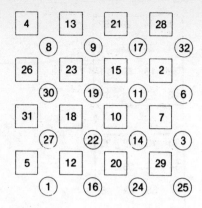

The Housing Development

8	1	14	11
10	15	4	5
3	6	9	16
13	12	7	2

No. 57

5	12	17	32
20	29	8	9
16	1	28	21
25	24	13	4

No. 58

10	7	18	31
19	30	11	6
15	2	23	26
22	27	14	3

36	19	25	18
37	6	48	7
24	31	13	30
1	42	12	43

47	26	20	5
14	11	41	32
29	44	2	23
8	17	35	38

21	34	39	4
27	16	9	46
10	45	28	15
40	3	22	33

No. 59

1	57	40	32
48	24	9	49
25	33	64	8
56	16	17	41

5	44	29	52
61	20	37	12
36	13	60	21
28	53	4	45

50	47	2	31
7	26	55	42
63	34	15	18
10	23	58	39

43	19	38	30
54	14	59	3
27	35	22	46
6	62	11	51

No. 60

47	2	49	32	15	34	17	64
30	51	46	3	62	19	14	35
1	48	31	50	33	16	63	18
52	29	4	45	20	61	36	13
43	6	53	28	37	12	59	22
54	27	44	5	60	21	38	11
7	42	25	56	9	40	23	58
26	55	8	41	24	57	10	39

The Knight Errant

1	48	31	50	33	16	63	18
30	51	46	3	62	19	14	35
47	2	49	32	15	34	17	64
52	29	4	45	20	61	36	13
43	6	53	28	37	12	59	22
54	27	44	5	60	21	38	11
7	42	25	56	9	40	23	58
26	55	8	41	24	57	10	39

No. 62

82

47	2	49	32	15	34	17	64
30	51	46	3	62	19	14	35
1	48	31	50	33	16	63	18
52	29	4	45	20	61	36	13
5	44	25	56	9	40	21	60
28	53	8	41	24	57	12	37
43	6	55	26	39	10	59	22
54	27	42	7	58	23	38	11

No. 63

1	48	31	50	33	16	63	18
30	51	46	3	62	19	14	35
47	2	49	32	15	34	17	64
52	29	4	45	20	61	36	13
5	44	25	56	9	40	21	60
28	53	8	41	24	57	12	37
43	6	55	26	39	10	59	22
54	27	42	7	58	23	38	11

No. 64

96	60	88	01	19
08	11	99	66	80
69	86	0	18	91
10	98	61	89	06
81	09	16	90	68

Topsy-Turvy

No. 66

8	10	15	1
13	3	6	12
2	16	9	7
11	5	4	14

8	13	2	11		11	5	4	14		14	7	12	1
3	10	5	16		16	2	7	9		9	4	15	6
9	4	15	6		6	12	13	3		3	10	5	16
14	7	12	1		1	15	10	8		8	13	2	11

1	15	10	8
12	6	3	13
7	9	16	2
14	4	5	11

14	4	5	11
9	7	2	16
3	13	12	6
8	10	15	1

No. 67

14	2	3	15
11	7	6	10
8	12	9	5
1	13	16	4

14	11	8	1		1	13	16	4		4	5	10	15
7	2	13	12		12	8	5	9		9	16	3	6
9	16	3	6		6	10	11	7		7	2	13	12
4	5	10	15		15	3	2	14		14	11	8	1

15	3	2	14
10	6	7	11
5	9	12	8
4	16	13	1

4	16	13	1
9	5	8	12
7	11	10	6
14	2	3	15

No. 68

8	13	12	1
2	11	14	7
9	4	5	16
15	6	3	10

8	2	9	15	15	6	3	10	10	16	7	1
11	13	6	4	4	9	16	5	5	3	12	14
5	3	12	14	14	7	2	11	11	13	6	4
10	16	7	1	1	12	13	8	8	2	9	15

1	12	13	8
7	14	11	2
16	5	4	9
10	3	6	15

10	3	6	15
5	16	9	4
11	2	7	14
8	13	12	1

No. 69

3	6	10	15
12	13	1	8
5	4	16	9
14	11	7	2

3	12	5	14	14	11	7	2	2	9	8	15
13	6	11	4	4	5	9	16	16	7	10	1
16	7	10	1	1	8	12	13	13	6	11	4
2	9	8	15	15	10	6	3	3	12	5	14

15	10	6	3
8	1	13	12
9	16	4	5
2	7	11	14

2	7	11	14
16	9	5	4
13	12	8	1
3	6	10	15

85

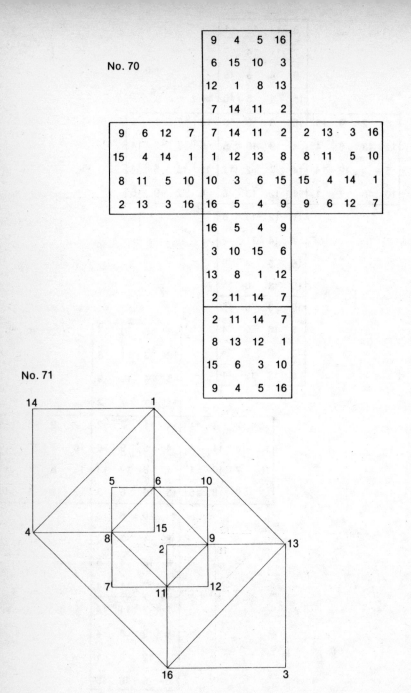

No. 70

				9	4	5	16				
				6	15	10	3				
				12	1	8	13				
				7	14	11	2				
9	6	12	7	7	14	11	2	2	13	3	16
15	4	14	1	1	12	13	8	8	11	5	10
8	11	5	10	10	3	6	15	15	4	14	1
2	13	3	16	16	5	4	9	9	6	12	7
				16	5	4	9				
				3	10	15	6				
				13	8	1	12				
				2	11	14	7				
				2	11	14	7				
				8	13	12	1				
				15	6	3	10				
				9	4	5	16				

No. 71

86

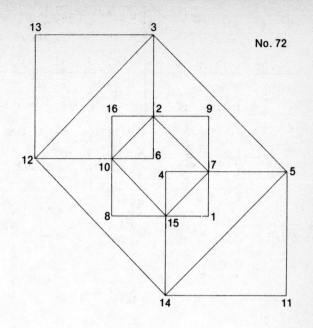

No. 72

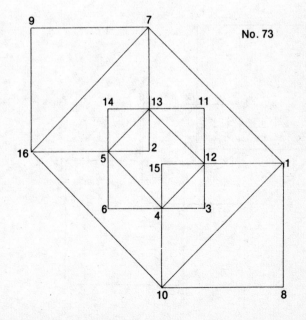

No. 73

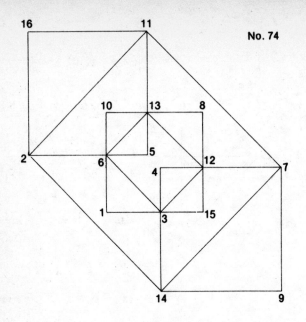

No. 74

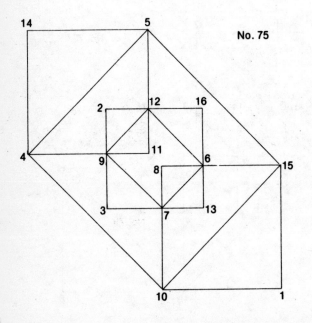

No. 75

88

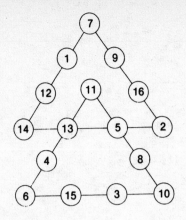

No. 76

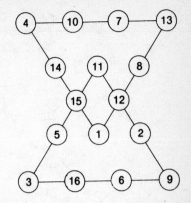

No. 77

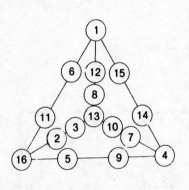

No. 78

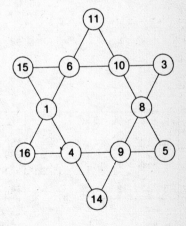

No. 79

89

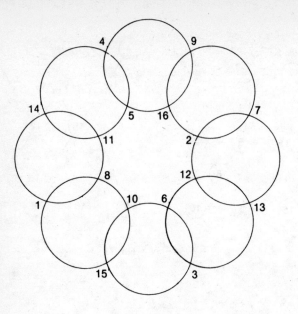

No. 80

10	3	6	15
5	16	9	4
11	2	7	14
8	13	12	1

No. 81

1	12	13	8
15	6	3	10
4	9	16	5
14	7	2	11

No. 82

1	15	10	8
12	6	3	13
7	9	16	2
14	4	5	11

MORE NUMBER PUZZLES

Contents

Introduction

Following on from 'Number Puzzles', this collection of puzzles is again based upon magic squares. Magic squares are squares comprised of different numbers, arranged in such a way that all the horizontal, vertical and both diagonal lines add up to the same total, or constant. Some magic squares possess these properties and no more, but for puzzle purposes the squares used must have further characteristics.

It may be useful here to set out all the groupings of 4 power and 5 power squares (that is, 4 × 4 squares and 5 × 5 squares) used in this book which produce the constant:

Regular 4 power squares
all horizontal lines
all vertical lines
both diagonals
the four quarters
the centre four squares
the four corners
the corners of the four 3 power squares contained within it
the centre squares, top and bottom
the centre squares, left and right
the two pairs of squares across diagonally opposing corners

A total of 24 groupings of four numbers, given three of which it is possible to derive the fourth.

Pan-diagonal 4 power squares
all the above, plus:
any four squares which together form a square
any corner square plus the three squares across the
opposing corner
A total of 32 groupings
Regular 5 power squares
all horizontal lines
all vertical lines
both diagonals
any symmetrical grouping of five squares which includes
the centre square
A total of 18 groupings of five numbers, given four of which it is
possible to derive the fifth.
Pan-diagonal 5 power squares
all horizontal lines
all vertical lines
both diagonals
any symmetrical grouping of five squares which includes
the centre square
any grouping of five adjacent squares in cross formation
(whether + or ×)
all broken diagonals (e.g. any corner square plus the four
squares lying across the opposing corner)
A total of 76 groupings, after transpositions.

As the reader will discover, some magic squares possess even
more amazing properties, and need not even be square-shaped!

With this further collection of puzzles I have attempted to
explore the versatility of magic squares a little further, and have
devised several new types of puzzle. These are no more difficult
than those in 'Number Puzzles', and like those puzzles can all be
solved by the application of simple addition and subtraction, plus,
of course, a little logic.

Happy puzzling!

1

The Careful Cashier

The hotel cashier was explaining the office routines to his new assistant.

"And here," he said, "we have the safe deposit boxes. Six of them, those that are numbered, are for our own use, and the other unnumbered ten are for the use of guests."

"Why aren't they numbered?" asked the new assistant.

"It's a security measure," replied the cashier. "The keys are numbered, and each one can only be inserted into one particular lock. If it is inserted into any other lock it is captured and a security bell rings in the duty manager's office. So if a guest loses his key, which does happen, it is extremely unlikely that a dishonest finder could use it to open the box, since he would have no means of knowing which box to go to."

"What is the point of numbering the keys if the boxes aren't numbered?" asked the assistant.

"The boxes are numbered," replied the cashier, "but the numbers are not displayed."

"If the numbers are not displayed, how do you know which key fits which box? Is there a chart somewhere?"

"No. That would reduce the security. You will have noticed that the numbers of the six hotel boxes appear to be in random order, but they are not. Their positions tell me exactly where each of the other boxes is. You see, the sixteen boxes are so arranged in four

3

rows of four that the total number of each row, horizontally, vertically or diagonally adds up to 34. So do the totals of the four boxes forming each of the four quarters, and the centre four boxes. There is sufficient information in the position of our six boxes to enable me readily to work out which box carries which number whenever a guest asks to go to his box. Don't look so worried! You'll soon get the knack.''

The position of the numbered boxes is shown below. Would you be able to direct a hotel guest to his particular box?

Puzzle No. 1

6			16
	13	7	
			5
1			

At irregular intervals the cashier rearranges the position of the hotel boxes as an additional security measure. The diagrams below show the last four such changes. Can you number the guest boxes?

Puzzle No. 2

1			
13	16		
	5		
		7	6

Puzzle No. 3

5			
16		7	1
	13		6

4

Puzzle No. 4

		5	16
7			
			13
6			1

Puzzle No. 5

13	1		16
			5
	7	6	

The five puzzles above can all be solved from the clues given, namely that the horizontal, vertical and diagonal lines, the four quarters and the centre four squares, all produce a constant of 34; but if you are stuck, remember also that the four corners, the centre squares, top and bottom, the centre squares, left and right, the four corners of each of the four 3 power squares contained within the square, and the two pairs of squares across diagonally opposing corners, all produce the constant.

All 4 power squares comprising the consecutive numbers 1 to 16 produce a constant of 34.

2

The Controlled Experiment

"Clever chap, that new superintendent at the Horticultural Gardens," said Albert, a gardener there, to his drinking companions. "He came up to me this morning and said, 'Albert, I want you to help me with a controlled experiment. We've successfully propogated this new strain of Allium and now we must find the best conditions for its cultivation. I've put the seedlings into these sixteen pots,' he said, 'each one containing a different number of plants from 1 to 16, because I want to see how they fare in groups of different sizes. I've arranged the pots in a square on this rack in such a way that they all get the same amount of air. If you look you'll see that every row, up and down and across, even diagonally, and every group of four pots which form a square, contains exactly 34 plants. Now, what I want you to do, Albert,' he said, 'is this. Every hour during the morning, take the row which is in the front and move it to the back, and in the afternoon when the sun has come round, take the left hand row and move it over to the right. In this way all the plants will receive the same amount of sunlight and at the end of a week or two we shall see how the plants like being together in groups of different sizes'."

"But surely," said one of his companions, "when you move a row from the front to the back, or from the left to the right, you must break up the groupings of 34?"

"That's just what I thought at first," replied Albert, "so every time I moved a row today I counted all the groups, and dang me if they didn't continue to add up to 34. That's why I say he's a clever chap, that new superintendent.''

"Well, he certainly seems to know his onions," said another, and they all laughed.

The diagram below shows the number of plants in five of the pots. Can you determine the number in the other pots?

Puzzle No. 6

6			9
		14	
13			
			16

This puzzle is based upon a pan-diagonal magic square, that is, one which retains its magical properties even when any number of rows are transposed from the top to the bottom, or from the left to the right, or both.

Pan-diagonal 4 power squares continue to possess all the properties of regular squares and have the following additional characteristics: not only do the four quarters and the centre four squares produce the constant, but so also do any four squares which together form a square; further, any corner square plus the three squares across the opposing corner also produce the constant. Puzzles based upon pan-diagonal squares can therefore be solved with fewer clues than those needed to solve those based upon regular squares. Whenever pan-diagonal squares are used in this book, that fact will be stated.

Complete the following pan-diagonal squares to produce constants of 42, 50, 58 and 70 respectively.

Puzzle No. 7

9			
			15
	17	12	
			18

Puzzle No. 8

5			16
19			
	9		
			17

Puzzle No. 9

		13	
9			12
16			
			10

Puzzle No. 10

14		17	
			12
	16		
	23		

3

The Roman Frescoes

The archeological excavation of a Roman villa in Pompeii had reached an important stage. The last trace of volcanic ash had been removed from one of the chambers and the Professor in charge was studying the wall frescoes which had been revealed.

"Yes," he said to his assistant, "this was probably the sanctum of the local oracle, or soothsayer. You can see the fragments of magic squares still visible on three of the walls. The oracles from the time of Augustus onwards attached great importance to the magical qualities of these squares. It was their practice to choose one square which they considered particularly propitious and then depict its four rotations, one on each of the four walls. From this fragment you can see that this particular magic square was four by four and since the numbers 1 and 16 are both clearly visible we can tell that the magic total was 34. It is a pity that none of the squares is complete, as the Institute has a duty to restore all frescoes to their original design wherever possible."

"If these fragments are all rotations of the same square," said his assistant, "it may be possible to reconstruct them in their original form. I'll give it some thought."

The fragments she had to work upon are reproduced below. Can you reconstruct the original squares as she did?

Puzzle No. 11

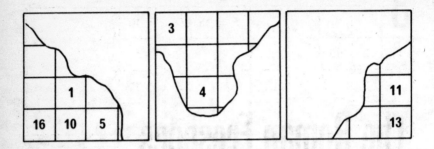

This puzzle requires a little more thought than those in Chapter 1, but it is nonetheless straightforward.

Four similar puzzles follow, all requiring completion to produce a constant of 34.

The solutions at the end of the book show the position of the first fragments unchanged, the second and third fragments being rotations.

Puzzle No. 12

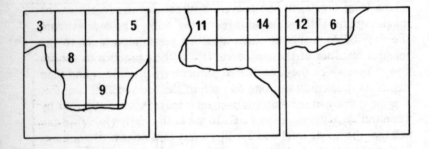

Puzzle No. 13

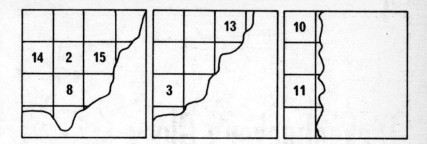

Puzzle No. 14

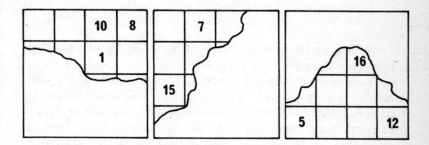

Puzzle No. 15

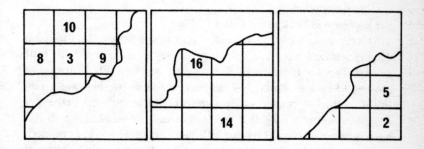

4

Rickenbacker's Glory

The Managing Director of Harridge's department store had called in his publicity man.

"Rickenbacker," he said, "we expect February to be a very poor month. You must think up something to get the customers into the store and spend their money. Something along the lines of a give-away, perhaps, something with flair, to create interest. Nothing extravagant, mind, because your budget will be limited to £4,000 or so."

"I'll get onto it right away, Chief, creation-wise," Rickenbacker said, and departed.

Later he was back in the Chief's office.

"I've got it, Chief," he said, "and it's a honey. In the main display window we put a slowly revolving glass cabinet with four glass shelves. On the corners of each shelf we put a different sum of money, £5 in one corner, £10 in another, £15 in another, and so on to £80 in the last corner. A big sign will tell the shoppers that every day the shopper who gets a receipt bearing the number which has been randomly selected by our in-house computer — programmed, of course, Chief, to be nearer the end of each day — will be allowed to go into the display window and select four piles of money, either all the money on any one shelf, or two adjacent piles of money and the two piles immediately above or below them, or any pile from the top shelf and the three piles immediately below it. Imagine the excitement, Chief! There'll be people outside the window shouting advice — choose those four! No! Choose those four! — Boy, will it create interest!''

"Rickenbacker," said the Chief, "have you gone mad? I said your budget was £4,000. Those shoppers aren't fools. They'll choose the four piles containing the greatest amount of money."

"Don't worry, Chief," said Rickenbacker. "I'll arrange the notes so that whichever piles are chosen the winner will always receive £170. Twenty-four shopping days at £170 will cost us £4,080."

"I hope you're right, Rickenbacker," said the Chief. "For your sake, I hope you're right. Otherwise you're fired!"

Rickenbacker works there still.

The diagram below depicts the four shelves of the glass cabinet. How had Rickenbacker arranged the bank-notes on the shelves so that the money at the corners of all 16 planes and the four vertical edges all added up to £170. The position and value of five piles are given.

Puzzle No. 16

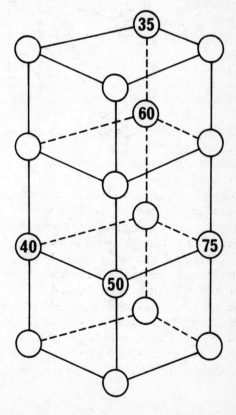

13

This puzzle utilizes the characteristic of a 4 power pan-diagonal square, namely that any four squares which together form a square, produce the constant.

Four similar puzzles follow, all requiring completion to produce a constant of 34.

Puzzle No. 17

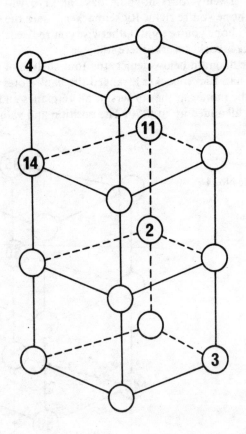

Puzzle No. 18

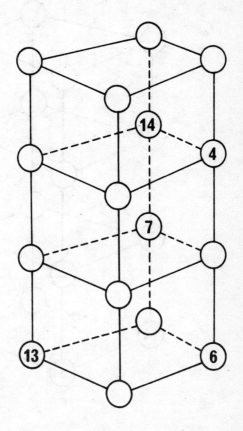

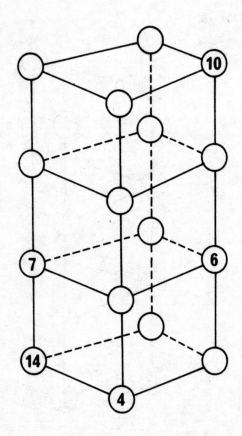

Puzzle No. 20

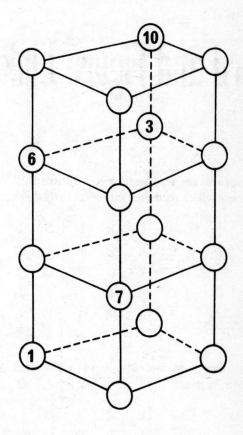

5

Word and Figure Link

Magic squares can also be formed with words, the more usual ones being those which read the same across and down, for example:

A	C	R	O	S	S
C	L	E	R	I	C
R	E	G	I	M	E
O	R	I	G	I	N
S	I	M	I	L	E
S	C	E	N	E	S

Others can be formed with words which read differently across and down, such as:

C	R	A	M
L	O	G	O
U	S	E	S
B	E	S	T

It is this latter type of word square which is used in the next five puzzles, since it can be converted to a figure square with the aid of an appropriate linking clue. For example, given the word square above and the linking clue:

Native of Bulgaria = 9, 6, 16, 5, 10, 13

one knows that the letters of the word 'BULGAR' (for that is the solution to the clue above) correspond to the above figures. If one then places those figures in a 4 × 4 grid in the squares which correspond to the positions occupied by the letters, the following incomplete figure square is revealed:

	13	10	
16		5	
6			
9			

With the knowledge that the constant is 34, it is relatively easy to complete the figure square:

3	13	10	8
16	2	5	11
6	12	15	1
9	7	4	14

Thus the word square leads to a figure square, given a linking clue.

The following five puzzles all require the initial creation of a word square, using normal crossword clues, so as to arrive at a figure square with a constant of 34.

Puzzle No. 21

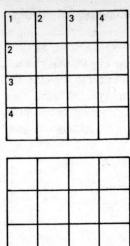

ACROSS
1 Spiders do.
2 Extreme dislike.
3 Always.
4 A short demonstration.

DOWN
1 Outhouse.
2 Cover with slabs.
3 Detail of news.
4 Roman fiddler.

LINK: Pungent root plant, eaten in a salad = 6, 1, 2, 5, 16, 7.

Puzzle No. 22

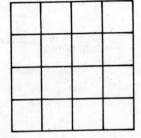

ACROSS
1 Large, graceful, long-necked bird.
2 Ring of light.
3 Preposition.
4 Day labourer in Central America.

DOWN
1 Vessel.
2 Diminish.
3 Counter-tenor.
4 Midday.

LINK: At the same time as = 14, 5, 10, 2, 4, 13.

Puzzle No. 23

ACROSS
1 --- scepter'd isle.
2 Competitive trial of speed.
3 The Bard's river.
4 House on a roof.

DOWN
1 Snare.
2 Possess.
3 Religious image.
4 Dispatched.

LINK: Twitters merrily = 10, 9, 16, 8, 11, 7.

Puzzle No. 24

ACROSS
1 Scottish tribe.
2 It springs eternal.
3 Wild mountain goat.
4 Examine critically.

DOWN
1 Written note.
2 Part of the ear.
3 Copies.
4 Following.

LINK: Religious chessman = 8, 12, 4, 14, 2, 15.

Puzzle No. 25

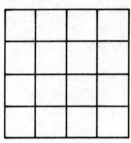

ACROSS
1 Taps backwardly.
2 Robust.
3 Common metal.
4 Necessary want.

DOWN
1 Climb — up a leg?
2 Peel.
3 Bitter purgative drug.
4 Watch over.

LINK: Impart a shine, not necessarily Slavonic = 6, 8, 14, 2, 15, 12.

6

The Maths Master

The Head was addressing the new maths master.

"I have just heard that the School Inspector is paying us a visit later today and will be testing one boy in five in your class. He is a strange chap whose practice is to select one row of boys, either horizontally, vertically or diagonally across the class-room. Now last year he chose the front row where your predecessor had placed all the duffers and as a result we didn't get a very favourable report. We don't want that to happen again, so do you think that you could move the boys around a bit so that there's a chance that the boys he tests will represent a more or less fair cross-section of the class?"

"I can do better than that," said the maths master. "I have already graded the boys in order of merit, the cleverest being No. 1 and so on down to No. 25. I will position them throughout the room so that whichever row the inspector chooses he will be testing an absolutely average cross-section of the class, neither better nor worse."

How did he do it? The position and grading of 8 of the boys is given.

Puzzle No. 26

4	20			11
18			1	
9			21	
		10		

This puzzle is based upon a regular 5 power magic square. Such a square comprising the numbers 1 to 25 has a constant of 65. In addition to the normal magical characteristics that the horizontal, vertical and diagonal lines produce the constant, these squares also have the property that any symmetrical grouping of five squares which includes the centre square also produces the constant.

In solving regular 5 power magic square puzzles it is useful to know that the centre square is always occupied by the mean figure, and that each pair of diametrically opposed numbers always total twice the mean.

Four further puzzles follow, requiring completion to produce constants of 70, 80, 90 and 100 respectively.

Puzzle No. 27

		26		15
5				3
	7	4		
				19

Puzzle No. 28

	11	9		
14			20	17
	26			
	7			

Puzzle No. 29

	28	11		22
	27			7
				30
	12			

Puzzle No. 30

28	26			18
8				
11			24	
		25		

7

The Coin Collection

"It is my wish," read the Last Will and Testament of the late Solomon King, "that my coin collection remain in the family, being divided equally between my five sons to add to their individual collections. In saying this I am conscious of the promise I made to my eldest son that he would always have first choice from my collection; also to my second son that he would always have second choice; and likewise to my third and fourth sons. I do not wish the division of the collection to become a source of friction and have therefore made the following arrangements. I have assessed the value of each of the twenty-five trays of coins and have numbered them according to their relative values, 25 to the most valuable, 24 to the next, and so on down to 1, the least valuable. I have positioned the trays, which my sons shall be at liberty to inspect, in the coin cabinet in a precise order.

"I now make the following specific bequests.

"To my eldest son I bequeath any five trays of coins of his choice which form a horizontal, vertical or diagonal row in my coin cabinet, or any five adjacent trays which together form a cross.

"To each of my other four sons I bequeath five trays of coins to be selected in the same manner as that adopted by my eldest son, the selections to be made by each son in turn in order of seniority.

"If my eldest son should choose five trays in a diagonal line or in cross-formation, my other sons may reposition the trays by moving any number of rows from the left to the right, or from the top to the bottom, or do both, provided that they can still make their choice by the same configuration. Such repositioning will not affect the evenness of the division as the numbers of all such groupings will continue to total 65.

"By these means I am ensuring that all my sons receive an equal portion of my collection, while at the same time I am honouring the promises I have made to my eldest sons."

When the five sons opened the doors of the cabinet they were dismayed to discover that most of the numbers had become unstuck and only 8 of them still adhered to the trays.

"So much for the Old Boy's weird idea," said one. "Now what do we do?"

"We study the situation calmly," said another, "and see if it is possible to work out where the other numbers go. We all know what Dad had in mind when he wrote about friction, so let's avoid it if we can."

They could and they did.

The diagram below shows the position of the eight numbers which remain adhered to the trays. Can you allocate the other numbers?

Puzzle No. 31

3		22		
	10		1	
				8
	23		17	
	19			

This puzzle uses the special characteristics of the pan-diagonal 5 power square, namely that any number of rows may be transposed from the left to the right or from the bottom to the top without destroying the square's magical qualities. Since the rows can be so moved, it follows that the mean figure can occupy any square, and not just the centre square. It also follows that diametrically opposed numbers no longer total twice the mean, as they do in regular squares.

Further characteristics of the pan-diagonal 5 power square are, first, that any grouping of five adjacent squares in cross-formation, (whether + or ×) also produces the constant; and secondly that so also do the broken diagonals (e.g. the two squares and three squares lying across opposing corners).

In solving these puzzles it may be necessary mentally to transpose rows in order to recognize groupings containing four of the five numbers.

A further four puzzles follow, requiring completion to produce constants of 65, 75, 85 and 95 respectively.

Puzzle No. 32

	25			
	2	10		
20				
	14		18	
3				15

Puzzle No. 33

	6	24		
		8		16
			20	
21		4	13	

Puzzle No. 34

		14		
			18	
15		6		
			10	8
12			21	

Puzzle No. 35

	26		15	
20				23
	28			14
	19		8	
				21

8

5 Power Number Jigs

The following puzzles are equivalent to jigsaw puzzles, the repeated numbers providing the clues as to where the sequences of numbers overlap or interlock.

In the first four puzzles you are required to arrange the sequences of numbers, some horizontally and some vertically in the adjacent grid in such a way that all the horizontal, vertical and diagonal lines add up to 65.

The fifth puzzle is harder in that the sequences could also be inserted in the grid diagonally.

All the squares are pan-diagonal, and some numbers have already been provided as clues.

16, 4, 12, 25.
14, 22, 10, 18.
8, 2, 21.
15, 23, 6.
21, 20, 14.
15, 9, 3.
23, 17, 11.
5, 24, 18.
25, 19, 13.
13, 7, 1.

Puzzle No. 36

	15			
			5	
	22			

8, 21, 14, 2.
12, 16, 25, 4.
13, 17, 21.
21, 1, 10.
6, 15, 19.
12, 5, 18.
24, 3, 17.
10, 23, 11.
7, 11, 20.
9, 22, 15.

		13		
	22			
		19		

2, 6, 18, 25.
7, 13, 19, 1.
15, 17, 3.
14, 16, 5.
2, 23, 9.
20, 24, 12.
5, 22, 8.
9, 11, 20.
21, 10, 12.
15, 4, 7.

			22	
		17		
		21		

20, 8, 1, 14.
4, 12, 25, 18.
7, 23, 4.
24, 5, 16.
20, 11, 7.
5, 13, 21.
16, 9, 2.
17, 10, 3.
19, 15, 6.
22, 3, 19.

	24			
		21		
22				

18, 14, 10, 1.
3, 16, 9, 22.
24, 20, 11, 7.
7, 4, 21.
4, 25, 16.
17, 13, 9.
8, 17, 1.
6, 2, 23.
24, 12, 5.
23, 19, 15.

24				
	21			
				22
	2			

9

6 Power Number Jigs

The following five puzzles are similar to those in the previous chapter but are based upon 6 power magic squares, comprising the numbers 1 to 36, and having a constant of 111. As with the 5 power number jigs, the sequences of numbers have to be inserted into the adjacent grids either horizontally or vertically, except that the fifth puzzle is harder, because the sequences of numbers could also be inserted in the grid diagonally.

Each line must total 111, and some numbers have already been provided as clues.

4, 19, 18, 33, 12.
30, 15, 22, 7, 24.
25, 36, 16, 20.
21, 17, 9, 24.
4, 6, 29, 10.
2, 34, 5, 28.
10, 32, 30.
20, 1, 13.
2, 14, 26.
23, 11, 3.
5, 8, 27.
35, 3, 31.

Puzzle No. 41

25					
			23		
		26			
				24	

Puzzle No. 42

16, 9, 19, 22, 28.
21, 29, 23, 14, 8.
18, 15, 35, 20.
5, 25, 24, 32.
20, 10, 26, 11.
8, 30, 36, 4.
31, 1, 33.
11, 27, 17.
34, 12, 13.
32, 6, 28.
2, 31, 34.
35, 7, 3.

		18			
	34			3	
8					

Puzzle No. 43

8, 26, 12, 29, 21.
24, 1, 17, 19, 36.
28, 34, 10, 4.
24, 5, 22, 13.
4, 31, 2, 9.
16, 23, 7, 21.
14, 30, 16.
6, 11, 25.
33, 3, 27.
13, 32, 15.
6, 35, 33.
20, 18, 2.

	28				
			25		
		20			
15					

Puzzle No. 44

17, 9, 21, 12, 28.
11, 2, 26, 20, 35.
1, 5, 33, 9.
14, 19, 36, 15.
7, 27, 3, 6.
11, 29, 23, 18.
14, 16, 7.
18, 8, 22.
10, 4, 31.
34, 30, 10.
13, 6, 24.
25, 32, 13.

34

	34				
		14			
18					
		13			

23, 31, 26, 12, 6.
4, 24, 15, 33, 22.
16, 2, 20, 25.
35, 6, 7, 32.
23, 34, 11, 18.
16, 36, 21, 14.
25, 35, 13.
9, 29, 27.
1, 31, 8.
18, 3, 22.
9, 30, 5.
17, 19, 28.
8, 10, 28.

			25		
	9				
				32	
	1				
			18		

10

The Measuring Device

"I say, Jack," said Sam to his friend and colleague at the Aerospace Laboratories. "Do you remember that measuring device I dreamed up some little while back?"

"Not really," said Jack. "Remind me."

"Well, it was for measuring the changes in temperature, potential and so on, in components under stress. Basically it was a series of micro-sensors set out as in these layout drawings. The sensors were linked in four different series; first, all sensors along the same circumference; secondly, all sensors along the same radius; thirdly, all sensors forming part of the same clockwise spiral; and lastly, those forming part of the same anti-clockwise spiral. All the sensors were linked to the computer which recorded and assessed any variations between the readings of the various sensor linkings during testing, and so it was easy to calculate the origin, extent and location of any hot-spots or weaknesses."

"Yes, I remember it now," said Jack. "So what's the problem?"

"Well, the number and position of the sensors has to be varied, depending upon the size of the component being tested. Sometimes it's 16, sometimes 25, or 36, 49, 64, or even 81 for the really big ones. What's happening is that when the sensors are changed, errors are being made in linking up the new sets of sensors, and so we're getting false readings. The Old Man's just told me I've got to make it idiot-proof, or else! You're the brains around here. Any ideas?"

Jack studied the layouts for a while, then said, "It's easy. Number all the sensors consecutively and feed that information into the computer. Then before each test, get a check-reading from the computer of the numerical link-up. If you don't get 16 readings of 34 when using 16 sensors, and 20 readings of 65 when using 25 sensors, and so on, then you know the linking is incorrect. Mind you, you'll need to work out all the various positions in advance. I'd work them out for you, but I haven't really got time. I'll start each one off for you, though, and leave you to finish them. O.K.?"

Each of Jack's seven incomplete layouts is shown below. As you go through them one by one, you will see the problem facing Sam and be able to pit your wits against his in arriving at a satisfactory completion of each one.

Puzzle No. 46

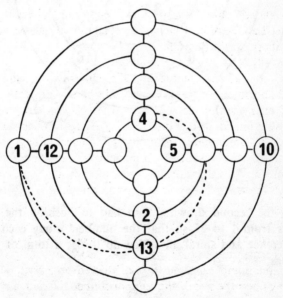

For the first layout drawing above Sam was required to position the missing numbers from 1 to 16 in such a way that the numbers along each radius, circumference and spiral, one of which is shown dotted, all added up to 34, giving 16 such groupings, or linkings.

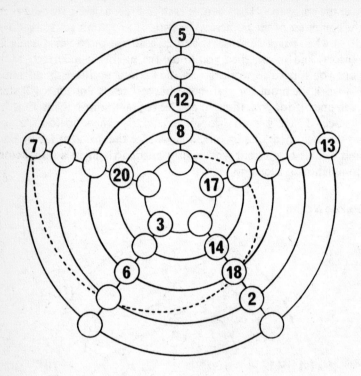

From the second drawing Sam had to position the missing numbers from 1 to 25 so that the numbers along each radius, circumference and spiral all added up to 65, a total of 20 such groupings.

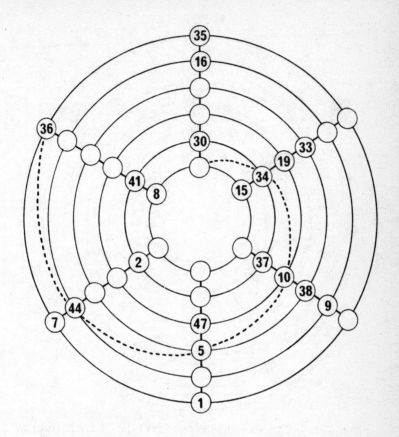

Sam found this layout a little harder to complete. He had to supply the missing numbers so that the numbers along each radius, circumference and spiral added up to 150, a total of 24 such groupings, but the numbers were not in a continuous series, being 36 of the numbers from 1 to 49.

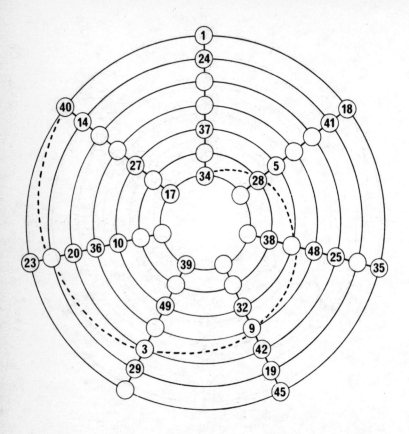

By the time Sam had reached this stage he was beginning to get the hang of it. He knew that he had to position the missing numbers between 1 and 49 in such a way that all the radii, circumferences and spirals added up to 175, a total of 28 such groupings, or linkings.

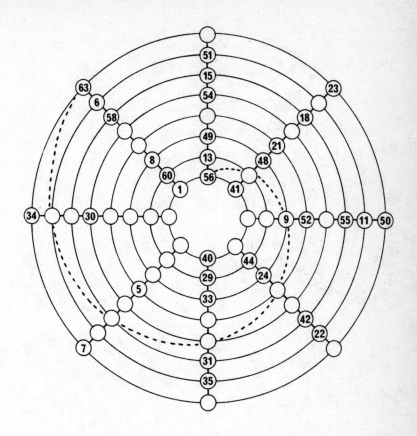

Sam found this layout drawing relatively easy to complete, because although he had to position the missing numbers between 1 and 64 in such a way that the totals of the numbers along each radius, spiral and circumference added up to 260, a total of 32 such groupings, Jack had told him that the totals half way along each radius was 130.

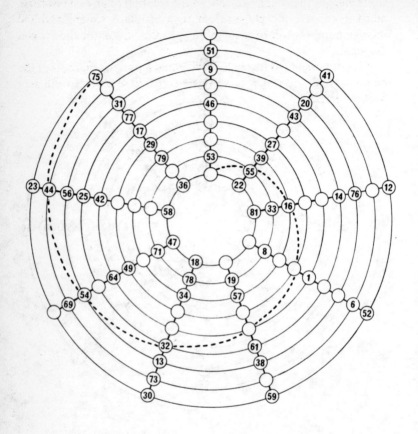

Sam completed his task by positioning the missing numbers from 1 to 81 so that the numbers along each radius, circumference and spiral, a total of 36 such groupings, added up to 369.

The measuring device had been made idiot-proof!

'Planetarium' puzzles such as these can be formed only from pan-diagonal squares. The radii correspond to the horizontal lines of the square, the circumferences or orbits correspond to the vertical lines and the spirals correspond to the diagonals and broken diagonals. So, in theory at least, they should be as easy to solve as standard magic square puzzles, but they appear not to be so. If you are really at a loss to find the solution to any one of these puzzles, convert the planetarium to a standard square and the missing numbers will become more apparent. Look for the broken diagonals.

It is not possible to form a pan-diagonal 6 power square from the numbers 1 to 36, which is why the series in Puzzle No. 48 is a broken series.

11

Magic Crystals

Using all the numbers from 1 to 16, supply the missing numbers in the following diagrams so that the corners of all seven rectangles contained within each magic crystal add up to 34.

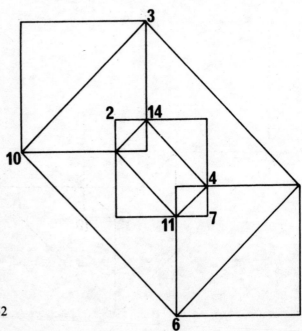

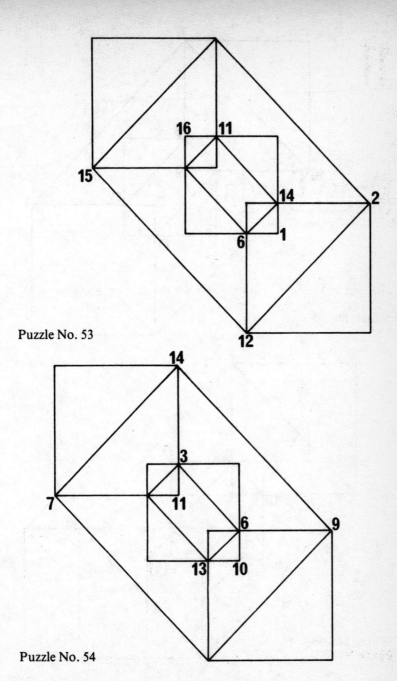

Puzzle No. 53

Puzzle No. 54

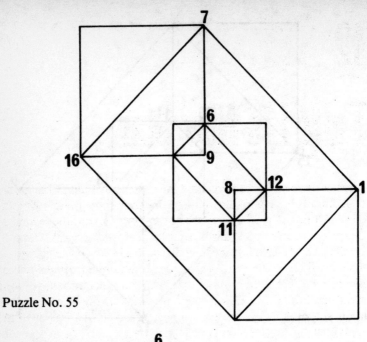

Puzzle No. 55

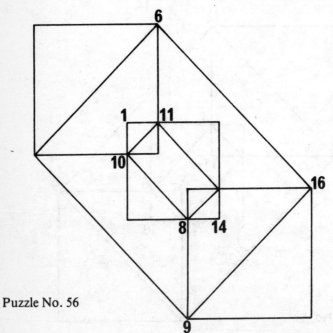

Puzzle No. 56

46

12

T'ang Li's New Star

Ancient manuscripts* tell of how the citizens of Liang Chang were once subject to an annual tribute of one pure sapphire to T'ang Li, the War Lord. The first sapphire was to be of 1 carat, the second of 2 carats, the third of 3 carats, and so on for as long as T'ang Li should live. After 25 years the citizens could no longer afford to make their tribute and, by a stratagem, had obtained their release by setting all the sapphires in a star for T'ang Li's turban, with the great sapphire of 25 carats in the centre and the others so arranged about it that in every direction, along every line, the weight of the sapphires was exactly 65 carats. Thus:

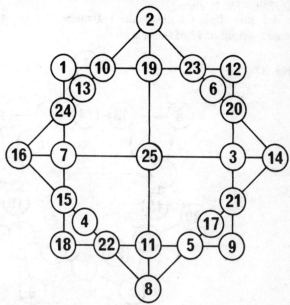

*see 'Number Puzzles', Chapter 7.

"I feel the bitter wind of penury throughout my palace," said T'ang Li to his chamberlain. "It is a matter of great regret that I absolved the citizens of Liang Chang from making their annual tribute these two years past. Had I not done so I would now possess two further sapphires, one of 26 carats and one of 27. With 53 carats weight of such gems I would have the means to gather and provision an army for another expedition, and thus replenish my coffers from the spoils of war. I have oft-times pondered upon the merits of prising some of the stones from the Star for that very purpose, but then my impoverishment would be visible to my enemies, and even worse, to my friends. Moreover, I dare not risk offending the Gods by destroying the mystical balance of the Star."

"Master," said the High Chamberlain, "disquiet yourself no further for I can perceive a way of removing the great sapphire and three others, weighing together 53 carats, and rearranging the gems in the form of another star, so that still in every direction, along every line, the weight of the sapphires is exactly 65 carats. Thus the Gods will continue in their approbation, and upon your victorious return neither friends nor enemies will have cause to question your great wealth."

How did the High Chamberlain rearrange the stones? The position and weight of 12 of them is given.

Puzzle No. 57

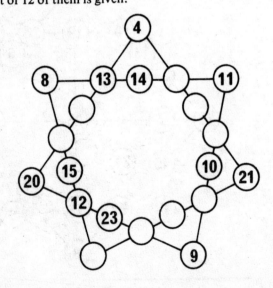

Four similar puzzles follow requiring completion to produce constants of 70, 80, 90 and 100 respectively.

Puzzle No. 58

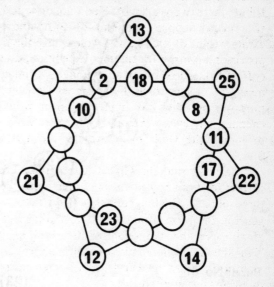

Puzzle No. 59

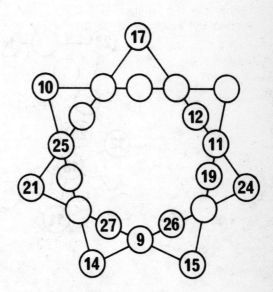

Puzzle No. 60

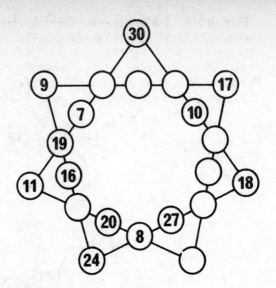

Puzzle No. 61

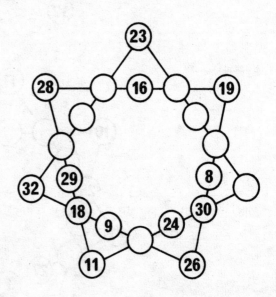

The original Star of T'ang Li was produced by a simple and fairly obvious variation of a pan-diagonal 5 power square. This new star is a further variation, but one not so obvious.

Had T'ang Li needed to take out 7 stones the High Chamberlain would no doubt have rearranged the Star as follows, still retaining the mystical total of 65.

Puzzle No. 62

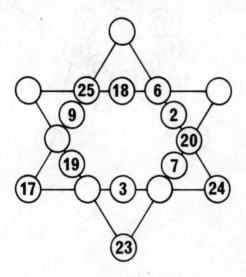

and had 10 stones been needed, the High Chamberlain could always have suggested the following, still retaining the mystical total of 65, which goes to show how versatile magic squares can be.

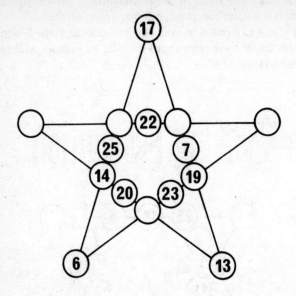

13

The Mindong Evacuation

A company of 450 Marine Commandos was beleaguered on the island of Mindong, and a worried C.O. was briefing his officers.

"At 05.30 hours," he said, "I received a long signal from Corps H.Q. informing me that an attempt will be made to airlift us off the island by helicopter troopships during the next five nights. It cannot be done quicker than that as 90 men each night is the maximum that the carrier can accept from us, bearing in mind that they are involved with other evacuations in the area, besides our own. Five helicopters have been specifically allocated to the task. Although each one can carry 90 men, H.Q. does not want to send in one helicopter each night to airlift the men in groups of 90, as this would mean exposing the helicopters in a vulnerable position on the ground for far too long, and also, to minimise losses in the event of enemy air-attack, they want us to remain dispersed over the island.

"So these are our instructions:

"On the first night we are to section off the island in a five by five grid pattern and position ourselves at pick-up points at the centre of each of the twenty-five sections. The five helicopters will approach under cover of darkness in line astern. They do not know the direction of their approach as this will largely be determined by enemy patrols and other activity in the area. As the pick-up points hear the helicopters approach, each will signal its position by flashlight. As they see these, the helicopters will land at the nearest line of five pick-up points — that could be horizontally, vertically or diagonally as one would look at it on the map — and airlift exactly 90 men back to the carrier. After clearance the men will transfer to one helicopter which will fly them back to the mainland and remain there.

"On the second night we are to section off the island in a four by four grid pattern and position ourselves at pick-up points at the centre of each of the sixteen sections. Four helicopters will approach under cover of darkness in line astern from an indeterminable direction. We will again signal our positions by means of flashlights and the helicopters will land at the nearest line of four pick-up points and airlift exactly 90 men back to the carrier. After clearance the men will transfer to one helicopter which will fly them back to the mainland and remain there.

"The process will be repeated on each of the following nights. On the third night we are to position ourselves at nine pick-up points in a three by three grid. Three helicopters will land at the nearest line of three, and airlift exactly 90 men to the carrier for transfer to the mainland. On the fourth night we are to position ourselves at four pick-up points in a two by two grid. Two helicopters will land at the nearest pair and airlift exactly 90 men to the carrier for transfer to the mainland. On the fifth night the remaining 90 men will collect at one pick-up point and be airlifted by the last remaining helicopter directly to the mainland."

As the C.O. paused, his second-in-command said, "If the helicopters are to pick up exactly 90 men each trip it would seem to indicate that we must position ourselves uniformly at each pick-up point, yet we know that there are parts of the island where the terrain will not permit more than 6 to 8 men to be positioned and still allow a helicopter to land. In any case, if 90 men are airlifted the first night, there is no way we can uniformly distribute 360 men over 16 pick-up points on the second night. So it is clear that we must distribute ourselves in a random pattern, but this carries the risk that the helicopters could land at groupings containing less than 90 men, and if this happens it would mean some men would be forced to stay on the island and take their chances, for there is no way of making up any shortfalls."

The C.O. said, "The final part of the signal set out the exact positions we were to take up, but our batteries were just about run down by this time and we were only able to receive snatches of the last part of the transmission. I've given what we did receive to Intelligence to try to fill in the gaps. I only hope they come up with the answer in time for us to position the men tonight."

He need not have worried. When the enemy invaded the island six days later, it was completely deserted.

The following diagrams were built up from the parts of the signal which were received and given to Intelligence to work upon. What solution did they arrive at?

Puzzle No. 64

		26		12
	25			29
30			28	
	19			16

	28		21
22			16
24		17	

28	30	
		27

Magic squares of different powers can be related in a variety of ways, and this puzzle demonstrates one of them, namely that squares of different powers can produce the same constant from consecutive numbers taken from the same series. The constant in this puzzle can be termed the Lowest Common Constant for squares of the 3rd, 4th and 5th powers.

Four other puzzles which demonstrate the relationship between squares of different powers, follow.

The first comprises an 8 power square, which encloses a 6 power square, which encloses a 4 power square, with constants of 260, 195 and 130 respectively. The 4 power square conforms to the normal rules and is the first one which should be solved. The numbers utilised are 1 to 64.

Puzzle No. 65

	52		56		12		58
63		18		42		49	
		25			32	20	64
59	41			27			
				40		44	8
14	22		28		35		
55			48		46		
		60		54		3	

The second comprises a 3 power square within a 5 power square within a 7 power square within a 9 power square, with constants of 123, 205, 287 and 369 respectively. The numbers utilised are 1 to 81.

Puzzle No. 66

5		11		10		12		
67			28		23			
	64	47		48				75
73			40			36	58	
	63	32		41	37			16
6						33	57	
	65		52		53			14
8		21		22		55	56	
	1		4		2		3	

The third puzzle involves distributing the numbers 1 to 50 between squares of the 3rd, 4th and 5th orders, as in the grids below, and producing from them magic squares with constants of 42, 91 and 157 respectively.

1	2	3
13	14	15
25	26	27

4	5	6	7
16	17	18	19
28	29	30	31
37	38	39	40

8	9	10	11	12
20	21	22	23	24
32	33	34	35	36
41	42	43	44	45
46	47	48	49	50

2		
	14	1

4			19
		6	
		40	
	7		30

49	45		21	
33	22			41
		42		
43		24		47
20	9		44	36

Puzzle No. 67

The last puzzle in this chapter demonstrates that it is possible to distribute a series of consecutive numbers between a square of one power and a square of one higher power, both producing the same constant.

In this puzzle the series 70 to 110 is used, and the constant of both the 4 power square and the 5 power square is 410. Both are pan-diagonal.

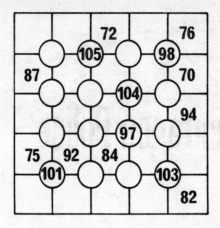

14

The Pentagon Police

It is common knowledge that the Pentagon in Washington is so named because of the shape of the building complex. What is not widely known is that the corridors within the complex are so arranged that they divide the building into eight separate pentagons, with a security control post located at each point and intersection, 15 in all, as set out in the diagram below. By a long-standing Army Ordinance the security police force of 300 men has to be deployed so that at all times a force of 100 men are positioned at the corners of each of the eight pentagons, so as to meet any emergency within that section. Until recently this Ordinance was satisfied by the simple and logical expedient of positioning 20 men in each of the control posts.

However, at the routine military briefing in the Oval Office last July, the President said to the Army Chief of Staff, "About the security police in the Pentagon, General. I'm not so sure that it is wise to position them so uniformly throughout the complex. Any enemy infiltrating the building knows exactly where they are and in what strength. I think you should redeploy them so that no two control posts contain the same number of men."

'Mr. President," said the General, "if it is possible to do that without breaching the Ordinance I will of course carry out your wishes. If not, I'll have to report back to you."

He did not have to.

The number of men in 8 of the control posts is shown, and although for reasons of military security no additional information can be given, any enemy infiltrator worth his salt should be able to work out the rest.

Puzzle No. 69

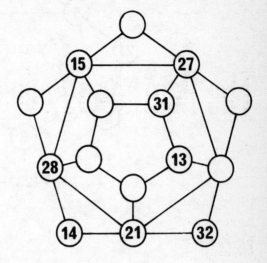

Four similar magic pentagon puzzles follow, requiring completion to produce constants of 70, 80, 90 and 100 respectively.

Puzzle No. 70

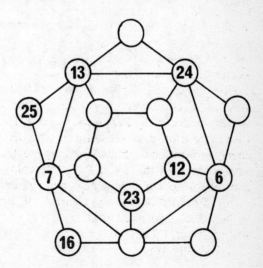

Puzzle No. 71

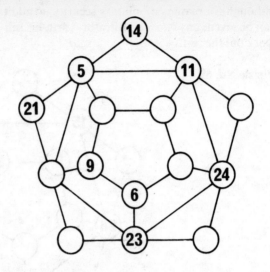

Puzzle No. 72

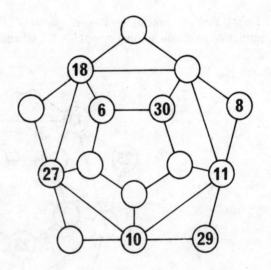

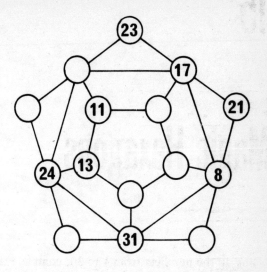

15

Magic Hexagons

Using all the numbers from 1 to 30, complete the magic hexagons below so that the points of all 9 hexagons contained within each one add up to 93.

Puzzle No. 74

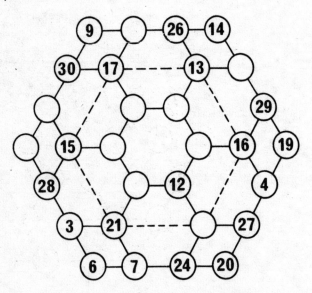

Puzzle No. 75

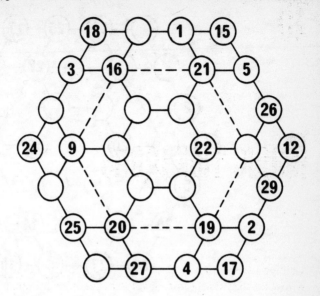

Puzzle No. 76

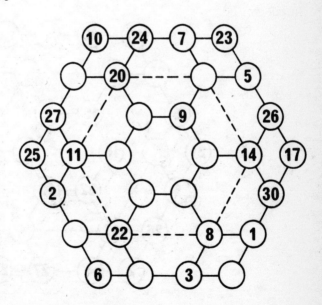

Puzzle No. 77

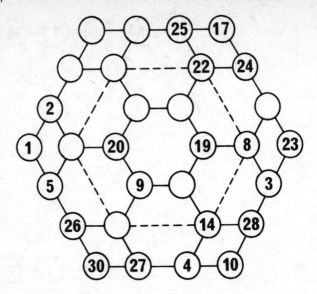

Puzzle No. 78

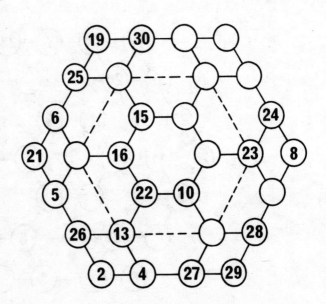

As we have seen, in a 6 power magic square comprising the numbers 1 to 36, the constant is 111.

Question: Why is it, when the numbers 31 to 36 are removed, as in the last five puzzles, the constant is reduced by only 18 and not by the average of 31 to 36?

16

The Incredible Adding Bee

When the ladies of the Oxbridge Entomological Society returned recently from their expedition to Central America they brought back five specimens of the hives of the Incredible Adding Bee (gen. apis arithmeticus) so named because of the precise numerical accuracy with which the Queen Bee deposits her eggs. She selects one empty hexagonal cell and in each of the six cells which surround it she deposits a different number of eggs. She continues in this fashion until she has filled 36 cells all containing a different number of eggs, and then starts the process over again. The incredible aspect of this ritual, the purpose of which is not yet understood, is that the eggs in the cells surrounding each empty cell always total exactly 111, despite the fact that each occupied cell can form part of three such groupings.

When the five specimens were unpacked it was discovered that the contents of several cells had perished in transit, but fortunately a sufficient number of cells survived intact to enable the ladies to ascertain the total number of eggs which were originally deposited in each cell.

From the following diagrams of the specimens as they were unpacked, can you supply the missing data?

Puzzle No. 79

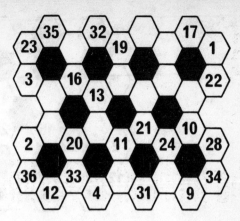

Puzzle No. 80

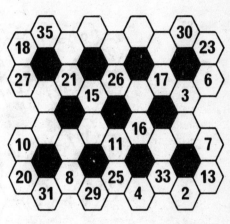

Puzzle No. 81

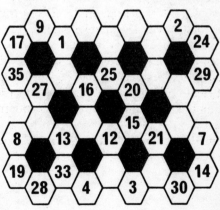

Puzzle No. 82

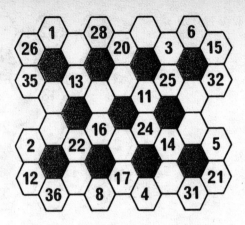

Puzzle No. 83

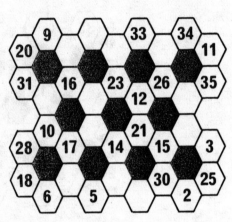

17

Magic Stars

It is possible to form magic stars of almost any size or complexity. The following puzzles set out a few in a progressive order, requiring completion to produce the constant shown in the centre of each respective star.

Puzzle No. 84

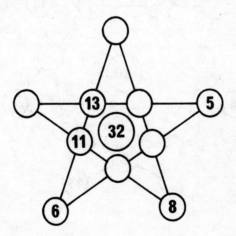

Puzzle No. 85

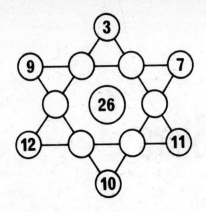

Puzzle No. 86

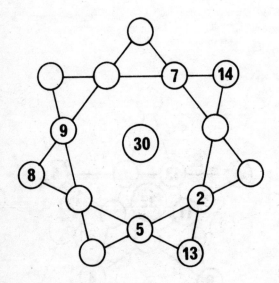

Puzzle No. 87

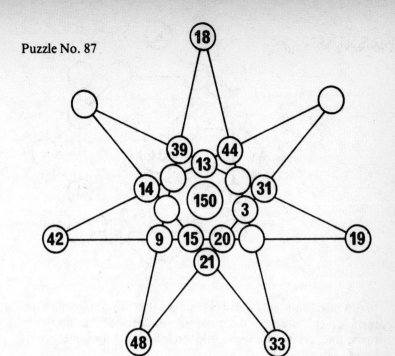

Puzzle No. 88

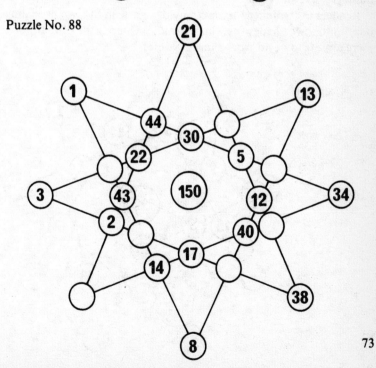

Puzzle No. 89

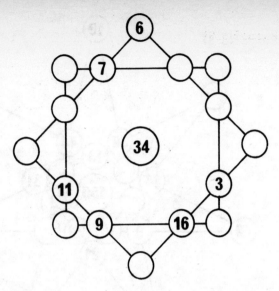

In this puzzle not only the lines produce the constant but also the corners of the squares, the pairs of numbers across opposing corners, the centre numbers, top and bottom, and the centre numbers, left and right.

Readers of 'Number Puzzles' may recognise in the two preceding puzzles the two shapes for which I said in Chapter 17 of that book there appear to be no cross-sums possible!

Puzzle No. 90

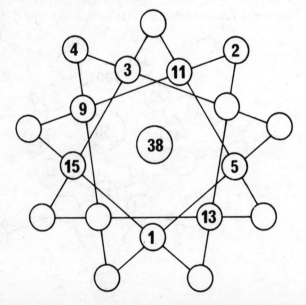

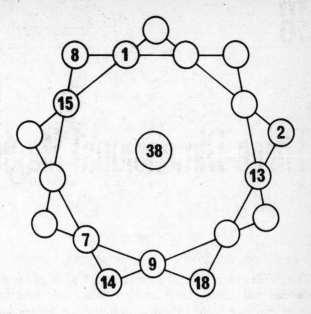

With the exception of Puzzles 84, 87 and 88, the puzzles in this Chapter all comprise the natural series 1 to n.

18

Three-Dimensional Magic

The puzzles in this Chapter demonstrate a few of the many three-dimensional arrangements possible with magic squares. The first three are three-dimensional in that they utilise solid forms, the arrangement of numbers being confined to the surface of those solids. The remaining puzzles are three-dimensional in the truest sense, the constants being produced from combinations which pass through the solids.

The first puzzle depicts a cube in two-dimensional form. Each of the six faces of the cube displays a different magic square, and all bordering squares have the same value as the squares they touch. Given one completed plane, one therefore has four clues for each of four other planes.

You are required to complete the cube to produce six magic squares each with a constant of 34. The second square down and the bottom square are both pan-diagonal.

Puzzle No. 92

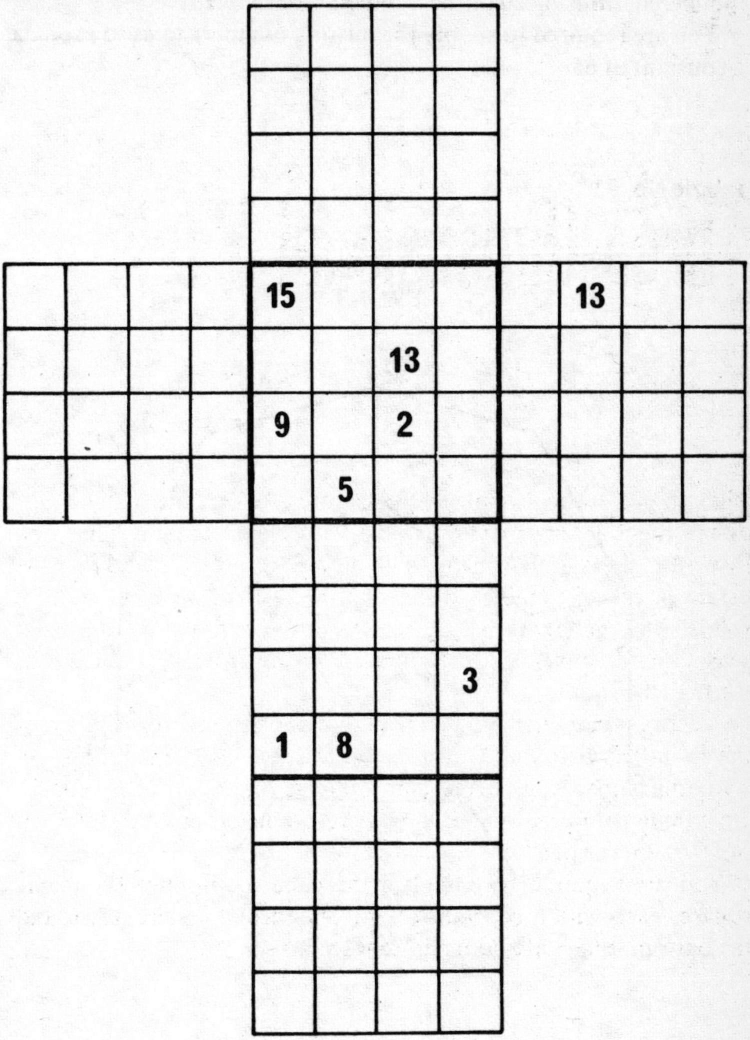

The diagrams below depict the front and rear views of a dodecahedron. The corners of the twelve pentagonal planes are numbered, utilising 20 of the numbers from 1 to 25.

You are required to supply the missing numbers so as to produce a constant of 65.

Puzzle No. 93

FRONT

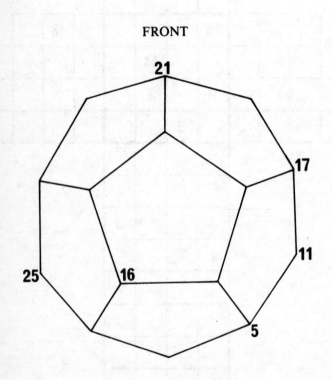

REAR

The diagrams below depict the front and rear views of an 'exploded' icosahedron comprising fourteen hexagons and six quadrangles. The corners of all fourteen hexagons are numbered consecutively from 1 to 36. You are required to supply the missing numbers to produce a constant of 111. Ignore the quadrangles.

Puzzle No. 94

FRONT

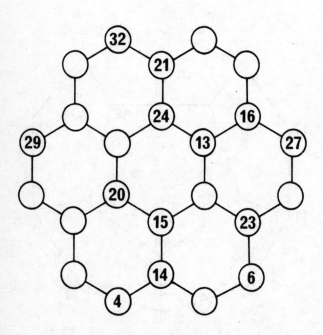

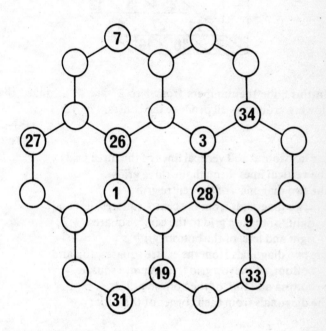

The diagram below shows a completed 3 power magic cube.

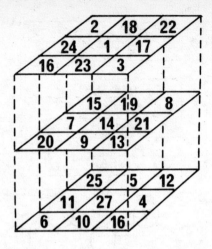

In this cube the numbers from 1 to 27 are so arranged that the following groupings all produce the constant of 42:

	No. of groupings
the horizontal and vertical lines of the three grids	18
the vertical lines through the three grids	9
the two diagonals of the centre grid	2
the two diagonals from the centre squares, left and right, of the top grid to the centre squares, right and left, of the bottom grid	2
the two diagonals from the centre squares, top and bottom, of the top grid to the centre squares, bottom and top, of the bottom grid	2
the diagonals from each corner of the cube	4
	37

The following two puzzles require the completion of similar 3 power magic cubes to produce a constant of 42 in each case. The five clues provided are sufficient to solve the puzzles without the need for trial and error.

Puzzle No. 95

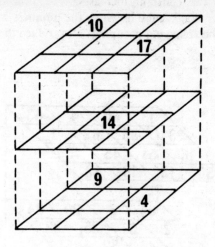

Puzzle No. 96

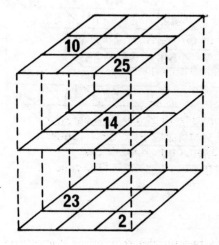

As one increases the size of the cube, so the number of groupings which produce the constant increases. The following diagram shows a 4 power magic cube in which the numbers 1 to 64 are so arranged that the following groupings all produce the constant of 130:

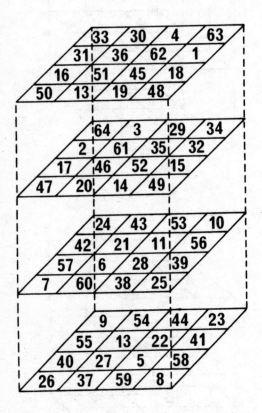

	No. of groupings
the horizontal and vertical lines of each of the four grids	32
the vertical lines through all four grids	16
the diagonals from each corner of the cube	4
the four quarters of each grid as depicted	16
the four quarters of each grid depicted when the cube is in its other two possible positions	32
	100

In order to make the less obvious groupings clearer, the following diagram shows four groupings, marked A, B, C and D, each of which produces the constant. Note that only the diagonals of the cube produce the constant. The diagonals of the individual grids do not.

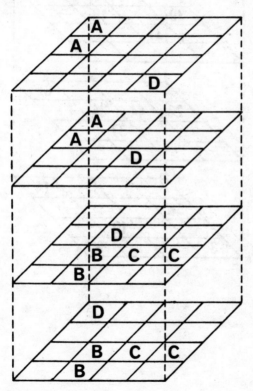

The following five puzzles involve similar 4 power magic cubes requiring completion to produce a constant of 130 in each case. The clues provided are sufficient to solve the puzzles without the need for trial and error.

Puzzle No. 97

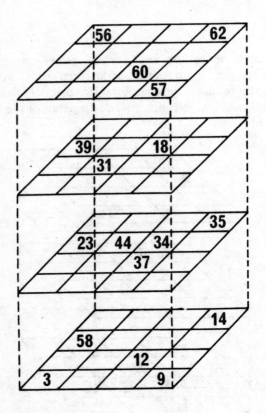

Puzzle No. 98

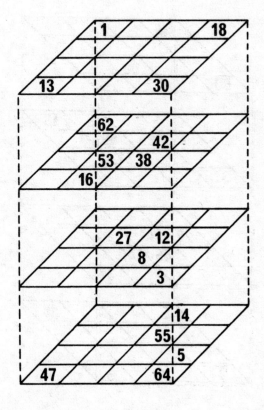

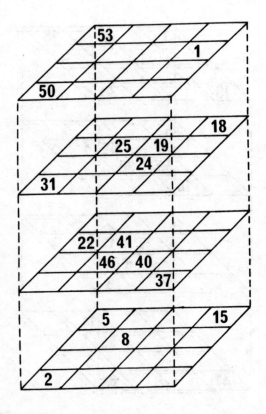

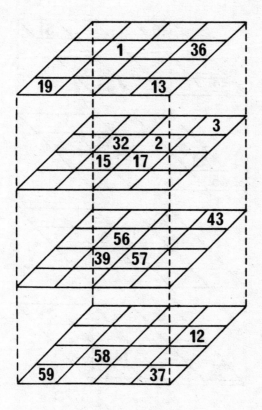

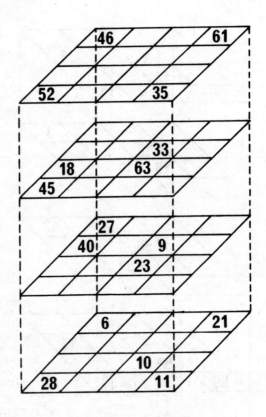

Solutions

6	3	9	16
12	13	7	2
15	10	4	5
1	8	14	11

1

1	4	14	15
13	16	2	3
8	5	11	10
12	9	7	6

2

5	3	14	12
16	10	7	1
11	13	4	6
2	8	9	15

3

11	2	5	16
7	14	9	4
10	3	8	13
6	15	12	1

4

13	1	4	16
8	12	9	5
11	7	6	10
2	14	15	3

5

6	15	4	9
12	1	14	7
13	8	11	2
3	10	5	16

6

9	16	13	4
14	3	10	15
8	17	12	5
11	6	7	18

7

5	18	11	16
19	8	13	10
14	9	20	7
12	15	6	17

8

22	8	13	15
9	19	18	12
16	14	7	21
11	17	20	10

9

14	20	17	19
25	11	22	12
18	16	21	15
13	23	10	24

10

2	8	11	13
9	15	4	6
7	1	14	12
16	10	5	3

11

3	10	16	5
13	8	2	11
6	15	9	4
12	1	7	14

12

7	11	6	10
14	2	15	3
12	8	9	5
1	13	4	16

13

5	11	10	8
14	4	1	15
3	13	16	2
12	6	7	9

14

13	10	4	7
8	3	9	14
11	16	6	1
2	5	15	12

15

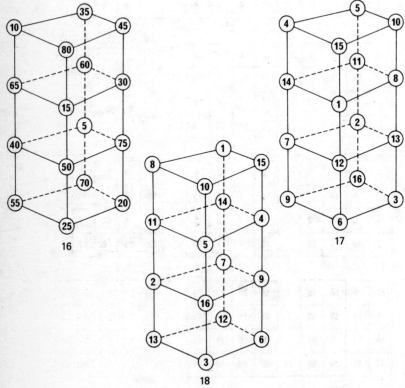

16

17

18

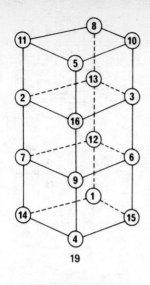

19

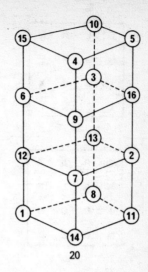

20

S	P	I	N
H	A	T	E
E	V	E	R
D	E	M	O

21

RADISH

16	10	5	3
7	1	14	12
9	15	4	6
2	8	11	13

S	W	A	N
H	A	L	O
I	N	T	O
P	E	O	N

22

WHILST

4	14	7	9
5	11	2	16
10	8	13	3
15	1	12	6

T	H	I	S
R	A	C	E
A	V	O	N
P	E	N	T

23

CHIRPS

2	9	16	7
8	15	10	1
13	6	3	12
11	4	5	14

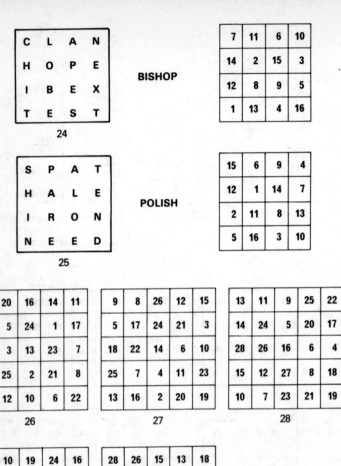

24

C	L	A	N
H	O	P	E
I	B	E	X
T	E	S	T

BISHOP

7	11	6	10
14	2	15	3
12	8	9	5
1	13	4	16

25

S	P	A	T
H	A	L	E
I	R	O	N
N	E	E	D

POLISH

15	6	9	4
12	1	14	7
2	11	8	13
5	16	3	10

26

4	20	16	14	11
18	5	24	1	17
19	3	13	23	7
9	25	2	21	8
15	12	10	6	22

27

9	8	26	12	15
5	17	24	21	3
18	22	14	6	10
25	7	4	11	23
13	16	2	20	19

28

13	11	9	25	22
14	24	5	20	17
28	26	16	6	4
15	12	27	8	18
10	7	23	21	19

29

21	10	19	24	16
6	28	11	23	22
29	27	18	9	7
14	13	25	8	30
20	12	17	26	15

30

28	26	15	13	18
8	16	17	30	29
31	21	20	19	9
11	10	23	24	32
22	27	25	14	12

3	11	22	9	20
24	10	18	1	12
16	2	14	25	8
15	23	6	17	4
7	19	5	13	21

31

9	25	13	1	17
11	2	19	10	23
20	8	21	12	4
22	14	5	18	6
3	16	7	24	15

32

14	23	22	11	5
12	6	15	24	18
25	19	8	7	16
3	17	26	20	9
21	10	4	13	27

33

23	16	14	7	25
9	27	20	18	11
15	13	6	29	22
26	24	17	10	8
12	5	28	21	19

34

29	26	18	15	7
20	12	9	31	23
11	28	25	17	14
22	19	16	8	30
13	10	27	24	21

35

8	16	4	12	25
2	15	23	6	19
21	9	17	5	13
20	3	11	24	7
14	22	10	18	1

36

12	16	25	4	8
5	9	13	17	21
18	22	1	10	14
6	15	19	23	2
24	3	7	11	20

37

14	16	5	22	8
2	23	9	11	20
6	15	17	3	24
18	4	21	10	12
25	7	13	19	1

38

20	11	7	23	4
8	24	5	16	12
1	17	13	9	25
14	10	21	2	18
22	3	19	15	6

39

24	20	11	7	3
12	8	4	25	16
5	21	17	13	9
18	14	10	1	22
6	2	23	19	15

40

25	4	19	18	33	12
36	6	2	34	5	28
16	29	14	23	8	21
20	10	26	11	27	17
1	32	35	3	31	9
13	30	15	22	7	24

41

21	2	18	15	35	20
29	31	1	33	7	10
23	34	12	13	3	26
14	5	25	24	32	11
8	30	36	4	6	27
16	9	19	22	28	17

42

24	1	17	19	36	14
5	28	34	10	4	30
22	6	11	25	31	16
13	35	20	18	2	23
32	33	3	27	9	7
15	8	26	12	29	21

43

11	2	26	20	35	17
29	34	1	5	33	9
23	30	14	16	7	21
18	10	19	25	27	12
8	4	36	32	3	28
22	31	15	13	6	24

44

16	2	20	25	35	13
36	9	29	27	6	4
21	30	17	12	7	24
14	5	26	19	32	15
1	31	8	10	28	33
23	34	11	18	3	22

45

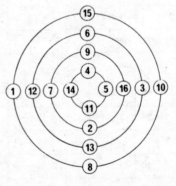

46

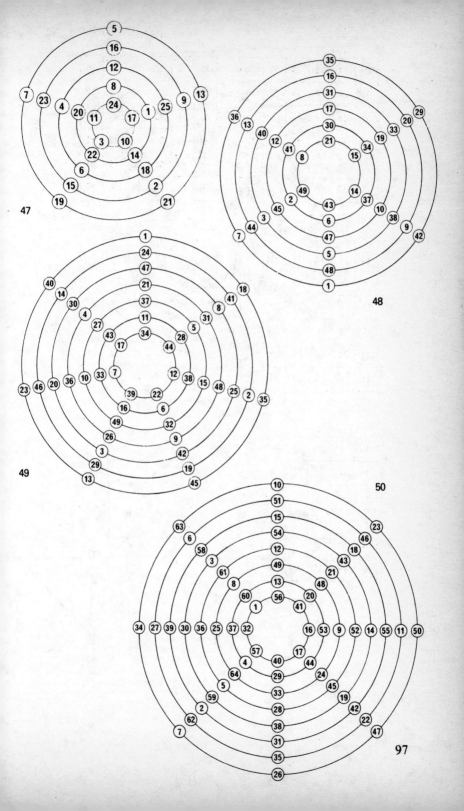

47

48

49

50

97

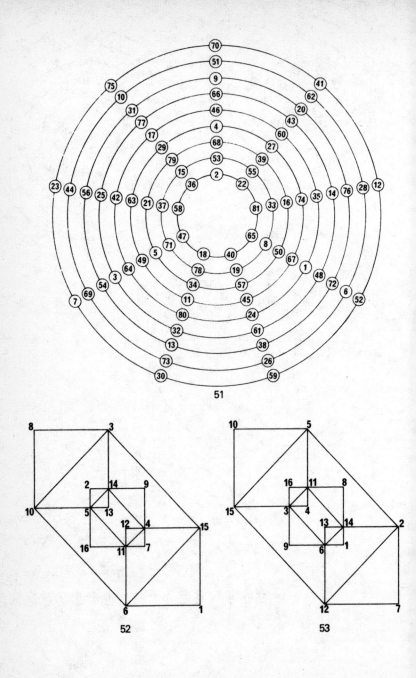

51

52

53

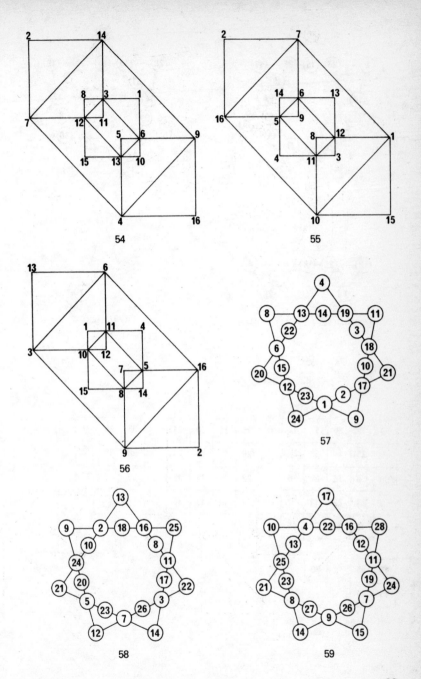

54

55

56

57

58

59

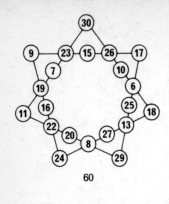

60

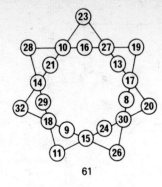

61

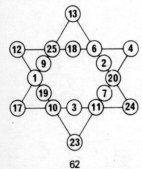

62

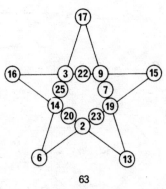

63

20	15	26	17	12
9	25	14	13	29
30	8	18	28	6
7	23	22	11	27
24	19	10	21	16

15	28	26	21
29	18	20	23
22	25	27	16
24	19	17	30

33	26	31
28	30	32
29	34	27

45	45
45	45

90

64

4	52	5	56	11	12	62	58
63	50	18	17	42	19	49	2
1	45	25	39	34	32	20	64
59	41	36	30	27	37	24	6
57	21	31	33	40	26	44	8
14	22	38	28	29	35	43	51
55	16	47	48	23	46	15	10
7	13	60	9	54	53	3	61

65

5	81	11	78	10	80	12	79	13
67	26	61	28	60	23	27	62	15
7	64	47	30	48	29	51	18	75
73	24	46	40	39	44	36	58	9
66	63	32	45	41	37	50	19	16
6	25	49	38	43	42	33	57	76
68	65	31	52	34	53	35	17	14
8	20	21	54	22	59	55	56	74
69	1	71	4	72	2	70	3	77

66

2	25	15
27	14	1
13	3	26

4	39	29	19
31	17	6	37
18	28	40	5
38	7	16	30

49	45	32	21	10
33	22	11	50	41
12	46	42	34	23
43	35	24	8	47
20	9	48	44	36

67

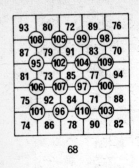

68

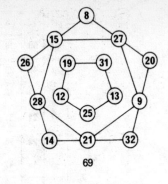

69

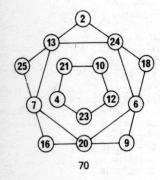

70

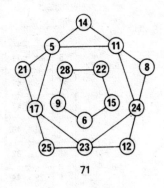

71

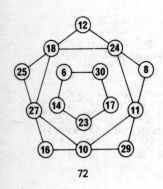

72

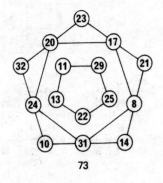

73

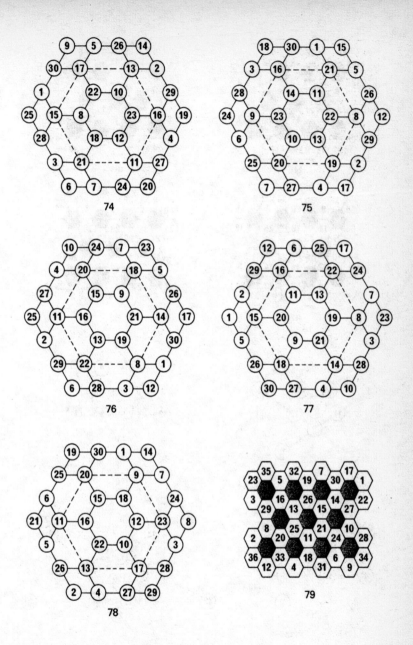

74

75

76

77

78

79

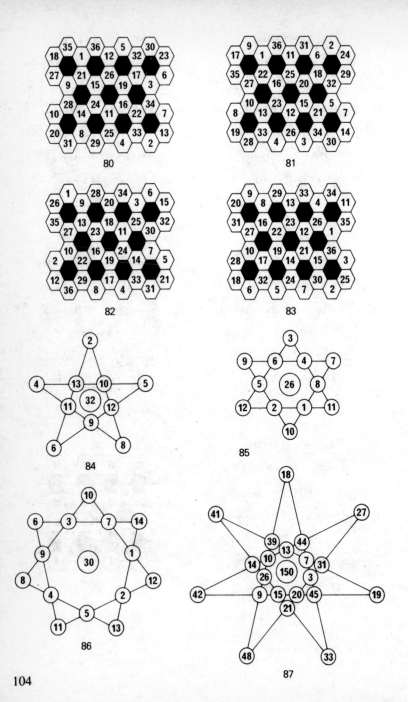

80

81

82

83

84

85

86

87

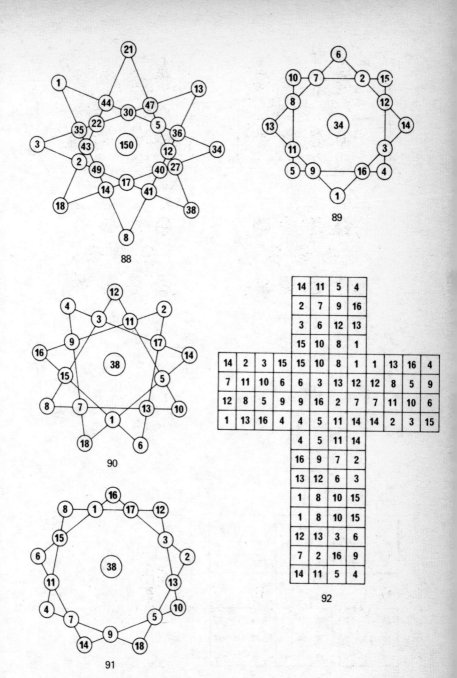

88

89

90

91

92

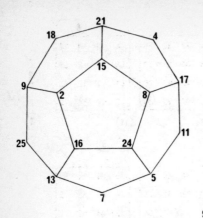
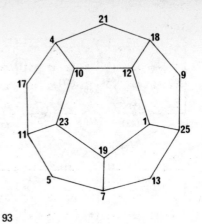

93

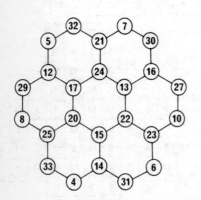
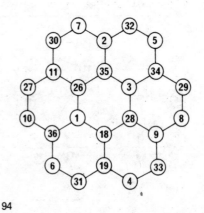

94

TOP

10	26	6		23	3	16		9	13	20
24	1	17		7	14	21		11	27	4
8	15	19		12	25	5		22	2	18

95

TOP

26	4	12		13	21	8		3	17	22
10	27	5		9	14	19		23	1	18
6	11	25		20	7	15		16	24	2

96

TOP

56	11	1	62
10	53	63	4
13	50	60	7
51	16	6	57

25	38	48	19
39	28	18	45
36	31	21	42
30	33	43	24

41	22	32	35
23	44	34	29
20	47	37	26
46	17	27	40

8	59	49	14
58	5	15	52
61	2	12	55
3	64	54	9

97

TOP

1	63	48	18
60	6	21	43
56	10	25	39
13	51	36	30

62	4	19	45
7	57	42	24
11	53	38	28
50	16	31	33

32	34	49	15
37	27	12	54
41	23	8	58
20	46	61	3

35	29	14	52
26	40	55	9
22	44	59	5
47	17	2	64

98

TOP

53	10	4	63
11	56	62	1
16	51	57	6
50	13	7	60

28	39	45	18
38	25	19	48
33	30	24	43
31	36	42	21

44	23	29	34
22	41	35	32
17	46	40	27
47	20	26	37

5	58	52	15
59	8	14	49
64	3	9	54
2	61	55	12

99

TOP

4	63	33	30
62	1	31	36
45	18	16	51
19	48	50	13

29	34	64	3
35	32	2	61
52	15	17	46
14	49	47	20

53	10	24	43
11	56	42	21
28	39	57	6
38	25	7	60

44	23	9	54
22	41	55	12
5	58	40	27
59	8	26	37

100

TOP

46	20	3	61
17	47	64	2
15	49	34	32
52	14	29	35

51	13	30	36
16	50	33	31
18	48	63	1
45	19	4	62

27	37	54	12
40	26	9	55
58	8	23	41
5	59	44	22

6	60	43	21
57	7	24	42
39	25	10	56
28	38	53	11

101

A Third Book of
Number Puzzles

Contents

Introduction

From the letters I have received from readers following the publication of *Number Puzzles* and *More Number Puzzles* it seems that magic squares still hold the same degree of fascination today as they have for centuries past. Attitudes, of course, have changed. At one time they were regarded superstitiously, as their name suggests. To Benjamin Franklin they represented an intellectual challenge. To some writers at the beginning of this century they epitomized the order, the harmony and symmetry which govern the natural laws of the universe. But there is nothing serious or pompous about magic squares; they are merely fun – a window opening upon a pleasant corner of the field of mathematics.

It is in such a spirit and context that I offer this third book, a further collection of puzzles, which attempts to explore the versatility of magic squares a little further.

For those readers who are new to them, magic squares are squares composed of different numbers arranged in such a way that the horizontal, vertical and diagonal lines add up to the same total or constant. The magic squares used in this book and its predecessors possess additional characteristics, however, which enable the constant to be obtained from several different groupings so that, for example, given three numbers in a group it is possible to derive the fourth by the application of simple arithmetic and a little logic.

The groupings of the four-power and five-power squares (that is 4 × 4 squares and 5 × 5 squares) which produce the constant are as follows:

Regular four-power squares
all horizontal lines
all vertical lines
both diagonals
the four quarters
the centre four squares
the four corners
the corners of the 4 three-power squares contained within it
the centre squares, left and right
the centre squares, top and bottom and
the two pairs of squares across opposing corners

7

These provide a total of 24 groupings of four numbers, given three of which it is possible to derive the fourth.

Pandiagonal four-power squares

all the above, plus:

any four squares which together form a square, and

any corner square and the three squares lying across the opposing corner

These provide a total of 32 groupings.

Regular five-power squares

all horizontal lines

all vertical lines

both diagonals, and

any symmetrical grouping of five squares which includes the centre square

These provide a total of 22 groupings of five numbers, given four of which it is possible to derive the fifth.

Pandiagonal five-power squares

all horizontal lines

all vertical lines

both diagonals

eight of the ten symmetrical groupings of five squares which include the centre square (the two non-conforming patterns are set out in Chapter 7)

any grouping of five adjacent squares in cross formation, whether upright (+) or slanting (×), and

all broken diagonals (that is, any corner square and the four squares lying across the opposing corner; and the two and three squares lying across opposing corners)

These provide, after transpositions, a total of 76 groupings.

As readers work their way through the book, they will become more and more familiar with the various groupings and will identify more readily those groups which are complete but for one number. To begin with, however, they will probably find it helpful to make frequent reference to the groupings listed above.

As in *More Number Puzzles* I have introduced some new shapes and configurations, for the versatility of magic squares means that they do not necessarily have to be square-shaped!

Happy puzzling!

Chapter One

The Uneven Load

The Despatch Manager called in one of his packers.

'We've got a problem, John,' he said. 'I was hoping to ship the sixteen crates you packed yesterday as a single consignment, but the freight company say that they can only accept single wagon loads when the weight can be evenly distributed. Since those crates range from 50 kilos to 200 kilos in 10 kilo increments, that seems to be out of the question, so I'd like you to open up the crates and redistribute their contents so that they all weigh the same. It means undoing work you've already done, but you won't be out of pocket. I'll allow you five bonus hours for the job'.

John thought for a while, then said, 'The freight company can load them as they are, and still get an even distribution of the load. Look.'

He drew a rough sketch and handed it to the Despatch Manager.

'If they load them like this in four rows of four, the weight of every row, left to right, back to front and diagonally, will be exactly 500 kilos. So also will the weight of the four crates in each quarter of the wagon and the four crates in the centre.'

'Well, I'm blowed,' said the Manager when he had checked that John was right. 'I would never have thought that possible. That was very smart of you, John. You've saved yourself a lot of work.'

'Yes,' replied John, 'but as you say, I'm smart, so I'll still take that five hours' bonus!'

The sketch below shows the weight of some of the crates as loaded into the wagon. Can you determine the weights of the others to produce the even load?

100	140		
			180
80			
130			160

Puzzle No. 1

This puzzle utilizes the characteristics of a regular four-power square and can be solved from the clues provided, but if you are in difficulty, remind youself of the many other groupings which produce the constant in regular squares.

Four similar puzzles follow, requiring completion to produce constants of 34, 50, 78 and 90 respectively. The numbers used in each square form a consecutive series.

4			
6	9		
	2		
		1	14

Puzzle No. 2

17			5
	6	18	
			10
8			

Puzzle No. 3

		12	18
16			
			13
15			24

Puzzle No. 4

21			
15		29	22
	19		25

Puzzle No. 5

10

Chapter Two

The Astonished Aunt

My Aunt Agatha, a noted numerologist in her day, once told me an amusing story concerning some workmen she had employed to redecorate her study. It appears that she had a favourite magic square in which the numbers 1 to 16 were so arranged that all the horizontal, vertical and diagonal lines totalled 34, and she wished this magic square and its three rotations (through 90°, 180° and 270°) to be depicted in her study, one on each of the four walls. She explained this to the workmen and gave them a diagram of each of the four squares. When they had gone to lunch, she looked in to examine their handiwork and found that their painting had reached the stage depicted below, with only two or three numbers having been painted in on three of the squares, the remaining wall being still completely blank. She picked up the diagrams to check the accuracy of their painting but absent-mindedly put them into her handbag instead of replacing them on the workbench. It was while she was out shopping much later in the afternoon that she discovered that she still had the working diagrams and immediately took a taxi home so that the decorators could continue with their work. Rushing breathlessly into the study she was astonished to find that, despite the absence of the diagrams, the workmen had successfully reconstructed all four squares and had completed their painting.

From the information given can you reproduce the magic square?

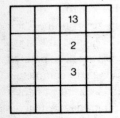 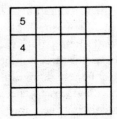 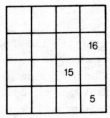

The top grids for Puzzle No. 6 contain:

12	13	1	

9	7		

8	10	11	

Puzzle No. 6

This puzzle requires a little more thought than those in the previous chapter, but arithmetically it is identical. Bear in mind the various combinations which produce the constant.

Four similar puzzles follow, all requiring the production of a constant of 34. The solutions at the end of the book show the first square of each puzzle but not the rotations.

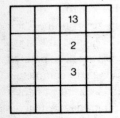 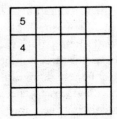 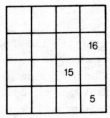

Puzzle No. 7

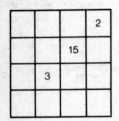 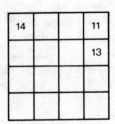 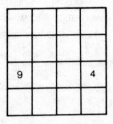

Puzzle No. 8

		8	10
		5	

	13		1

6			
11			

Puzzle No. 9

4			13
			10

	14	9	
		8	

	16	1	

Puzzle No. 10

Chapter Three

The Wisdom of Solomon

And there came a shepherd unto Solomon, saying, 'My Lord, three days past I did find a pot long hid beneath some rocks, and in this pot were two hundred pieces of gold. And my master, hearing of my find, said unto me, 'By ancient custom three-fourths belong to me, and but one fourth is thine.' But my master is rich and needs not the gold, whilst I am poor and in great need. Judge, O King, I pray you, that I may keep even all the gold.'

Now Solomon desired that all his people should honour the customs of their forefathers, yet desired not to seem unmindful of the sufferings of the poor. So he commanded that sixteen boxes be placed before him in four rows of four.

Then, turning to the shepherd he said, 'Thou shalt have whate'er the Lord God wills. See, I am placing five gold coins in this box, six in this box, seven in this, and thus unto twenty in this last box. Seeing now where all two hundred pieces lie, thou mayest choose for thyself the gold in any row, be it horizontal, vertical or diagonal.'

And the shepherd studied the boxes, then said, 'My lord, whichever row I choose it matters not, for they all contain fifty gold pieces.'

So the King said, 'Thou mayest then choose the gold in any four boxes which form a square.'

And the shepherd studied the boxes again, then said, 'My lord, all such squares contain exactly fifty gold pieces.'

'Then,' said the King, 'lest I be thought unjust, before thou choosest, thou mayest move any number of rows from the left to the right, from the bottom to the top, or even both.'

And the shepherd studied the boxes yet again, then said, 'O mighty King, no matter how I move the boxes I cannot change the number of

14

coins in any such grouping of four. Great is thy wisdom, for thou hast shown me that the ancient customs of our forefathers are founded upon eternal truths.'

'Take then thy fourth,' said the King, 'and be content.'

How had Solomon in his wisdom placed the coins? The contents of some of the boxes are shown below.

12	17		
		13	
	7		19

Puzzle No. 11

This puzzle is based upon a pandiagonal square, that is, one which retains its magical qualities even when rows are transposed from left to right, from top to bottom or both. Pandiagonal squares of the fourth power possess all the properties of regular four-power squares plus the further characteristics that the constant is also produced by any four squares which together form a square, and also by the broken diagonals, i.e. a corner square and the three squares lying across the opposing corner. These additional characteristics make it possible to solve pandiagonal puzzles with fewer clues. Whenever puzzles in this book are based upon pandiagonal squares, that fact will be stated.

Four further pandiagonal puzzles follow, requiring completion to produce constants of 34, 50, 70 and 90 respectively.

	3		
8			1
2		9	

Puzzle No. 12

	15		14
17			
		11	13

Puzzle No. 13

10			21
		18	
		11	22

Puzzle No. 14

20		21	
		25	19
	27		

Puzzle No. 15

16

Chapter Four

Grandfather's Pennies

It was always a delight when my grandfather visited us for tea for he was a very kindly old gentleman. After tea he would often perform little conjuring tricks which left us gasping with astonishment as when, for example, he would make coins seemingly disappear into thin air only to be retrieved from behind a small ear to the accompaniment of shrieks of pleasure.

I remember one visit vividly, for when we had finished eating he eyed the four-tiered cake-stand in the centre of the table, then said to my three brothers and me, 'I've brought you all some bright new pennies, but before you get them you must do some arithmetic. Watch carefully. In the corner of this tier I am placing one penny; in the corner of this tier, twopence; in the corner of this tier, threepence; and so on until in this last corner I am placing sixteen pence. Now, John,' he continued, 'you are the eldest so you may have first choice. You may choose any four piles of coins on the same tier; or any two adjacent piles of coins and the two piles immediately above or below them; or any pile from the top tier and the three piles immediately below it. Then the rest of you, in order of seniority, may each choose your four piles, using the same configuration as John. Then we will see who has chosen most.'

My youngest brother immediately looked very glum, for he had only just started school and was not very good at sums, but my grandfather, seeing this, put his arm around him and whispered, 'You think that the others will choose the piles containing the most pennies, don't you, so that when it comes to your turn you will be left with the least. Don't worry, Ian. It doesn't matter which piles the

17

others choose; at the end you'll find that you all have exactly thirty-four pence each.'

I do not know how he did it, but he was absolutely right.

The diagram below depicts the four-tier cake-stand showing the position and value of five piles of coins. How had my grandfather arranged the others?

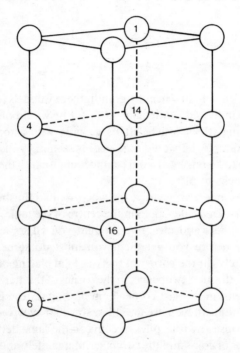

Puzzle No. 16

This puzzle utilizes the characteristic of four-power pandiagonal squares whereby the constant is produced by any four squares which together form a square.

Four similar puzzles follow. You are required to provide the missing numbers in a consecutive series to produce constants of 58, 62, 38 and 82 respectively.

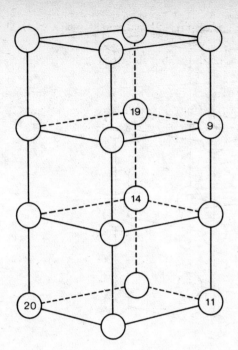

Puzzle No. 17

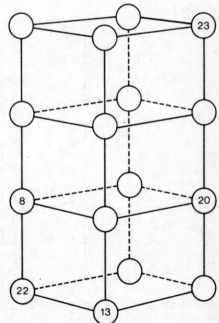

Puzzle No. 18

19

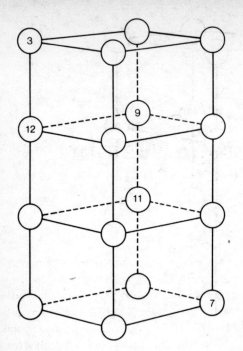

Puzzle No. 19

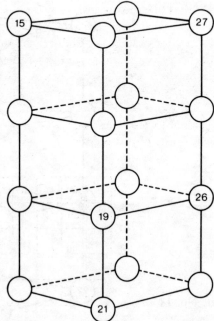

Puzzle No. 20

20

Chapter Five

The Average Weight

The form-master was addressing his class.

'The Head is arranging a tug-of-war competition between the three classes in this year, and to avoid any class putting up their five heaviest pupils he himself is going to select each team at random by choosing five boys in a row, either horizontally, vertically or diagonally across the classroom. Now, there is no point in my putting the five heaviest boys in one particular row hoping that the Head will choose that one, because, if he doesn't, we will have lessened our chances. So what I have decided to do is this. I will grade you all by weight, the heaviest being Number 1 and so on down to the lightest at Number 25. Then I will position you throughout the classroom so that, whichever row the Head selects, he will be choosing a perfectly average weight of boys.'

How did the form-master arrange the class? The position and grading of eight of the boys are given.

	20		22	
	25		21	
				17
24				
14				18

Puzzle No. 21

This puzzle is based upon a regular five-power magic square which, using the numbers 1 to 25 produces a constant of 65. In addition to the constant being produced by the horizontal, vertical and diagonal lines, it is also provided by any symmetrical configuration of five squares which includes the centre square. A further help in solving these regular five-power puzzles is that the centre square is always occupied by the mean figure, and each set of diametrically opposed squares totals twice the mean.

Four similar puzzles follow, requiring completion to produce constants of 70, 80, 90 and 100 respectively.

		4		26
7				5
	11			
	6	8		
				15

Puzzle No. 22

		6		
	18			19
	22			11
15			5	25

Puzzle No. 23

24				
29		8	19	
			10	
	23	14	21	

Puzzle No. 24

16			11	
32		10		12
				31
			21	
			18	

Puzzle No. 25

Chapter Six

Magic Stars

It is very easy to devise star patterns of almost any size or complexity, but it is not always so easy to work out the cross-sums! The following five puzzles utilize five of the more basic shapes. You are required to provide the missing numbers so as to arrive at constants of 30, 34, 38, 43 and 65 respectively. Apart from the fourth puzzle, they all comprise the natural series 1 to n.

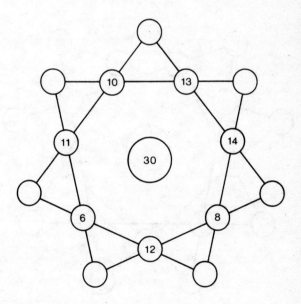

Puzzle No. 26

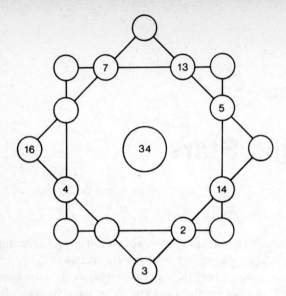

Puzzle No. 27

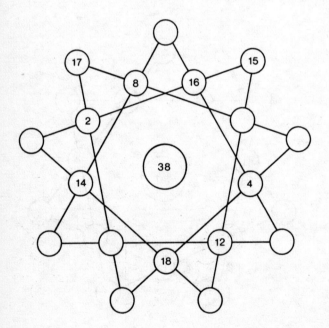

Puzzle No. 28

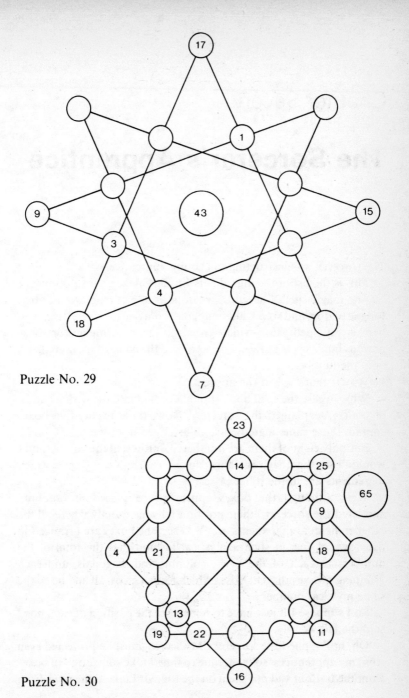

Puzzle No. 29

Puzzle No. 30

Chapter Seven

The Sorcerer's Apprentice

The sorcerer was instructing his young apprentice.

'This is the list of the ingredients I use to make up my potions for casting magic spells,' he said, 'eye of newt, toe of frog, wool of bat, tongue of dog, and so on, all numbered from one to twenty-five. And here is my spell book which gives the secret formulae for those potions but, as you can see, I never record the name of the ingredient, only the number.'

'Why is that?' asked the apprentice.

'Why, in case the spell book should ever fall into the wrong hands, of course,' explained the sorcerer. 'Now, these twenty-five boxes contain those same ingredients, all arranged in order.'

'But only eight of them are numbered,' protested the youth, 'and I wouldn't say that they're arranged in order, so how can you tell which ingredients are in the other boxes?'

'Well, although the boxes appear to be placed at random,' answered the sorcerer, 'their position tells me exactly where all the other individual ingredients are. You see, the boxes are arranged in five rows of five in such a mystical fashion that the total of the numbers in each of the rows, columns and diagonals, and each grouping of five adjacent boxes which form a cross, all add up to the same mystical number.'

'So I suppose I'll just have to remember the position of each box,' said the lad wearily.

'Oh, no!' replied the sorcerer. 'My secrets must be protected even from my apprentices, so from time to time I take some rows of boxes from the bottom and put them on the top. Or I take some rows from the right and transfer them to the left. Sometimes, when I'm feeling particularly peevish, I do both.'

'Doesn't that upset the groupings which add up to the mystical number?' asked the boy.

'Not at all,' replied the sorcerer archly. 'You will discover that I am a very superior wizard.'

'When will I be told what the mystical number is?' asked the apprentice.

'Whenever I think I have reached the age to retire,' replied the sorcerer.

'Sixty-five?' suggested the lad innocently.

'Curses! You've guessed!' screamed the sorcerer, vanishing in a puff of smoke never to be seen again.

With the smell of brimstone gradually dispersing, can you help the apprentice to number the unmarked boxes?

	17			
				16
		20	4	
	3			15
21		14		

Puzzle No. 31

This puzzle is based upon a pandiagonal five-power square. These squares have similar properties to regular squares, but in addition the constant can be obtained from any grouping of five adjacent squares in cross formation and from the broken diagonals. These additional properties make it possible to solve pandiagonal puzzles with the aid of fewer clues, but you may have to transpose rows or columns mentally in order to recognize further groupings which contain four of the five numbers. Since the rows and columns can be transposed, it follows that the mean need not occupy the centre square and that diametrically opposite squares need not total twice the mean.

Four similar puzzles follow with constants of 75, 85, 95 and 105 respectively.

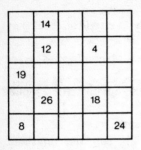

Puzzle No. 32

Puzzle No. 33

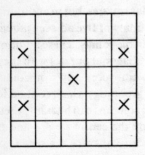

Puzzle No. 34

Puzzle No. 35

As was mentioned in the Introduction, there are two symmetrical groupings which do not produce the constant in five-power pandiagonal squares. They are shown below:

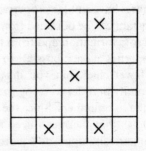

Chapter Eight

Five-power Number Jigs

The following puzzles are similar to jigsaw puzzles, the repeated numbers providing the clues to where the series of numbers link or overlap. In the first four puzzles you are required to insert the sequences of numbers into the grid either horizontally or vertically so as to produce a constant of 65. The fifth puzzle is slightly harder, since some sequences of numbers have to be inserted diagonally. All the squares are pandiagonal and some numbers are provided as positioning clues.

3, 19, 15, 6
13, 5, 7, 19
18, 25, 12
14, 1, 8
10, 21, 2
8, 20, 22
9, 16, 23
12, 4, 6
10, 17, 24
24, 11, 3

Puzzle No. 36

4, 8, 17, 21
2, 6, 20, 24
5, 9, 18
15, 7, 24
23, 12, 1
25, 14, 3
8, 25, 2
10, 13, 16
22, 11, 5
10, 19, 23

Puzzle No. 37

25, 8, 16, 4
15, 2, 19, 6
24, 18, 12
11, 10, 4
21, 20, 14
23, 17, 11
7, 1, 25
14, 22, 10
15, 9, 3
21, 13, 5

Puzzle No. 38

12, 5, 8, 16
11, 4, 7, 20
3, 6, 19
17, 11, 10
9, 23, 2
25, 13, 1
10, 24, 3
19, 22, 15
18, 12, 6
21, 14, 2

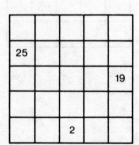

Puzzle No. 39

21, 10, 17, 3
8, 19, 1, 15
20, 11, 9
22, 6, 18
13, 7, 5
25, 16, 14
13, 24, 6
23, 17, 15
20, 4, 12
8, 2, 25

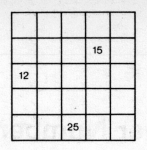

Puzzle No. 40

Chapter Nine

Six-power Number Jigs

A six-power magic square comprising the numbers 1 to 36 has a constant of 111. The following five puzzles are number jigs based upon such squares, and as in the previous chapter, you are required to insert the sequences of numbers into the grid so as to arrive at the constant. In the first four puzzles the sequences are to be positioned either horizontally or vertically, but in the fifth puzzle some of them must be positioned diagonally.

1, 35, 3, 7, 32
5, 34, 30, 2, 4
25, 4, 16, 13
11, 36, 22, 23
28, 8, 32, 10
24, 14, 31, 25
13, 33, 20
18, 27, 21
29, 12, 26
6, 5, 9
17, 19, 28
15, 10, 20

Puzzle No. 41

4, 24, 11, 33, 22
31, 8, 7, 36, 2
21, 18, 5, 23
14, 15, 29, 21
19, 26, 10, 12
28, 3, 6, 5
17, 27, 19
31, 9, 34
14, 25, 28
25, 20, 30
34, 1, 32
16, 13, 35

		28			
				30	
					32
	27				

Puzzle No. 42

34, 9, 30, 4, 29
8, 7, 33, 28, 32
23, 3, 12, 21
13, 16, 2, 22
17, 24, 5, 11
18, 1, 20, 25
2, 28, 6
26, 15, 30
27, 15, 14
35, 8, 31
10, 29, 36
26, 19, 6

	3				
			27		
13					
					25
			10		

Puzzle No. 43

30, 24, 14, 7, 17
1, 19, 16, 36, 26
23, 2, 20, 18
34, 15, 21, 3
5, 31, 4, 27
17, 22, 8, 12
13, 35, 18
10, 6, 33
30, 28, 5
11, 25, 9
33, 32, 29
9, 27, 34

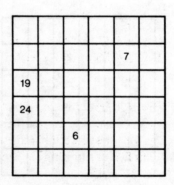

Puzzle No. 44

3, 31, 15, 28, 27
34, 2, 22, 9, 5
3, 16, 21, 34
20, 10, 18, 13
14, 36, 11, 26
24, 19, 32, 17
3, 29, 4
26, 1, 23
35, 8, 27
7, 33, 28
5, 30, 6
25, 12, 28

Puzzle No. 45

Chapter Ten

A Cautionary Tale

The professor in charge of the archaeological dig gently brushed the soil from the tablet his team had just uncovered.

'This is most interesting,' he said. 'It records that the Emperor was to pass in a straight line through the city on his thirty-eighth birthday and to honour the occasion the Governor, Numericus Fastidius, placed a different number of the Legion's 190 standards at each road intersection so that whichever route the Emperor chose for his imperial progress through the city, he would pass exactly thirty-eight standards. Then there is a diagram of the city showing the nineteen road intersections and the number of standards at each of them, though unfortunately, only six of them are clearly decipherable.'

He brushed some more soil away.

'Oh, dear!' he said, 'It then goes on to say that the Emperor was so flattered by the compliment that he returned on his following birthday, and when Numericus failed to repeat the tribute he had him thrown to the lions!'

The moral of this story is clear: before one first figures to please an unruly master, one must first please master the unruly figures.

The city diagram showing the six decipherable numbers is depicted below. Can you, without fear of furnishing a feline feast, provide the others?

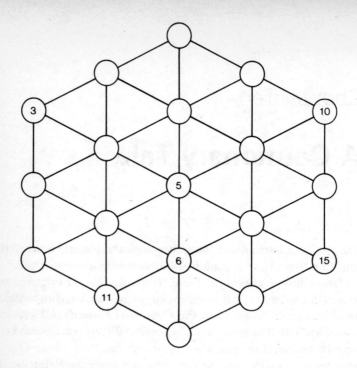

Puzzle No. 46

I wish I could set four further puzzles based upon this cross-sum, but, as poor old Numericus found to his cost, the configuration is unique, so this must perforce be the shortest chapter in the book!

Chapter Eleven

The Patent Solution

'Your late father was, as you know, a rather eccentric inventor,' said the solicitor to Peter, 'and among the residue of the estate which he has bequeathed to you is the patent specification relating to a combination mechanism for safes. It comprises thirty-two tumblers numbered from one to thirty-two. When the combination is first set these tumblers have to be inserted into four cog wheels in such a way that the numbers in each wheel total 132.'

'There's nothing patentable in that, surely?' asked Peter.

'No, but in addition every horizontal row of eight tumblers must also total 132...'

'Nor in that.'

'...and continue to do so even when the cog wheels are turned.'

'Good heavens! Is that possible?'

'It must be, since the patent has been incorporated into several safes. Unfortunately, when your father filed his patent application he deliberately omitted several of the numbers from the specification drawings in order to keep the relative position of the tumblers a trade secret. He kept the completed drawing securely locked away in his private safe, together with all his securities.'

'Well, then,' said Peter, 'let's look in there.'

'That's the problem,' said the solicitor. 'We can't open the darned thing until we have the combination!'

From the incomplete specification drawing shown below, could you open the safe? In solving this puzzle bear in mind that there are 16 positions for each cog wheel, not eight as one might initially believe. The constant of 132 is obtained from the horizontal lines of eight tumblers in all 16 positions, as well as from the eight tumblers in each cog wheel.

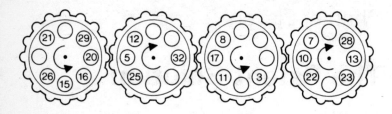

Puzzle No. 47

The versatility of magic squares is truly amazing. Magic cog wheels, indeed!

Four similar puzzles follow, all requiring completion to produce a constant of 132.

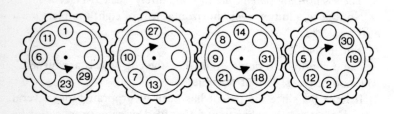

Puzzle No. 48

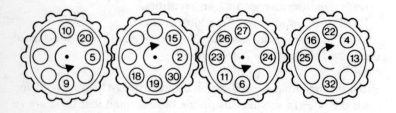

Puzzle No. 49

38

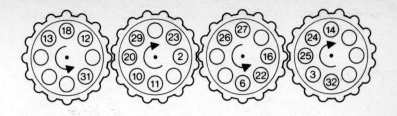

Puzzle No. 50

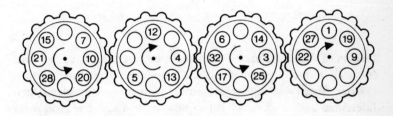

Puzzle No. 51

Chapter Twelve

Spheres of Influence I

Readers of *Number Puzzles* who recall the Kyrosian Tactic and the Zukarian Counter, have doubtless wondered from time to time whether those warring neighbouring planets ever resolved their differences and if so, how. It can now be revealed that, following protracted discussions on the Mutual Understanding Specifying The Activation of Retaliatory Defence (the MUSTARD Talks), the Supreme Councils of the respective planets reached an agreement under the terms of which each planet was permitted to station 351 astronauts in 26 killer/spy satellites in orbit around its neighbour. Despite this, suspicion still remained. Fearing that the Zukarians would bring their charged-particle-beam weapon to bear on all the satellites in one given orbit, the Kyrosians stationed a different number of astronauts in each satellite. They positioned their battle fleet in seven geostationary orbits around Zukar so that, should all the satellites in any particular orbit be destroyed, they would be left with exactly 243 astronauts in 18 satellites, sufficient to launch a successful retaliatory strike against Zukar itself.

The orbits of the satellites are shown opposite together with the manning levels of some of them. Can you determine the number of astronauts in the other satellites? The constant you are seeking is 108.

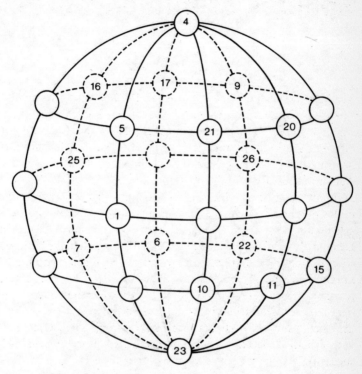

Puzzle No. 52

Four similar puzzles follow.

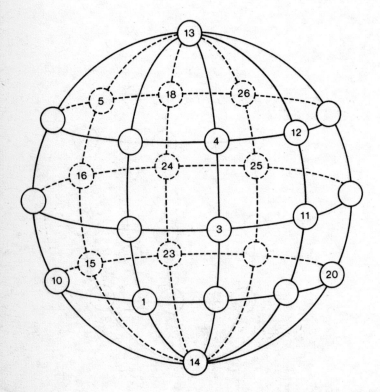

Puzzle No. 53

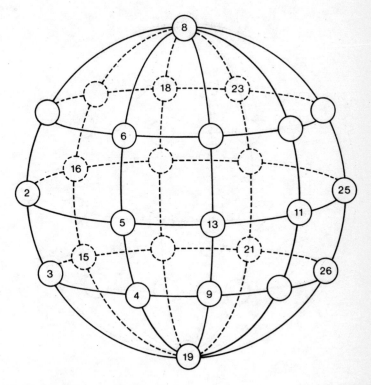

Puzzle No. 54

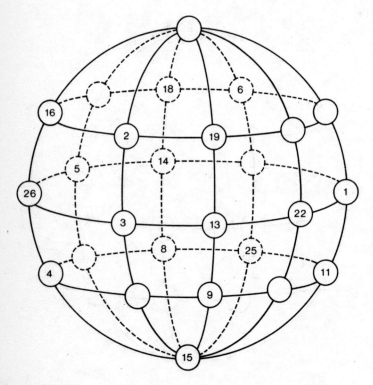

Puzzle No. 55

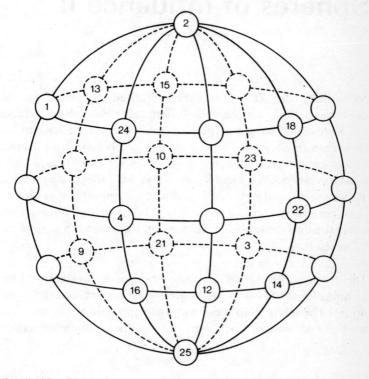

Puzzle No. 56

The solutions to these five puzzles provided at the end of the book are
not unique. There are alternatives.

Chapter Thirteen

Spheres of Influence II

Meanwhile, the Zukarians, who perceived the merit of the deployment of the Kyrosian battle fleet, being themselves fearful of the Kyrosians' charged-particle-beam weapon, sought to position their fleet to obtain the same degree of protection. Being a more sophisticated race, however, they positioned their fleet in nine geostationary orbits around Kyros so that, while they also would lose 108 astronauts and eight satellites should any one orbit be destroyed, they nevertheless gained the military advantage of forcing their adversaries to deploy more weapons on the ground to achieve the same result.

The orbits of their satellites are shown opposite, together with the manning levels of some. Can you determine the complements of the others? The solutions to these five puzzles provided at the end of the book are not unique. Some pairs of numbers are interchangeable.

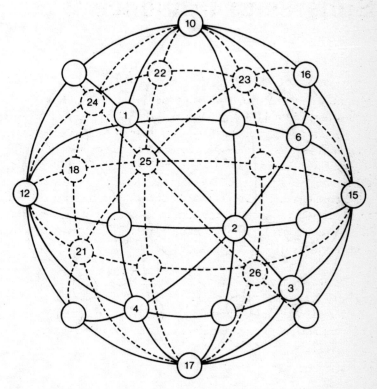

Puzzle No. 57

Four similar puzzles follow.

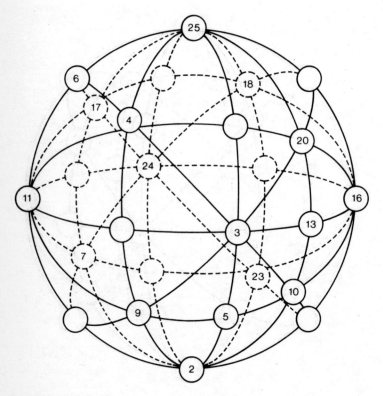

Puzzle No. 58

48

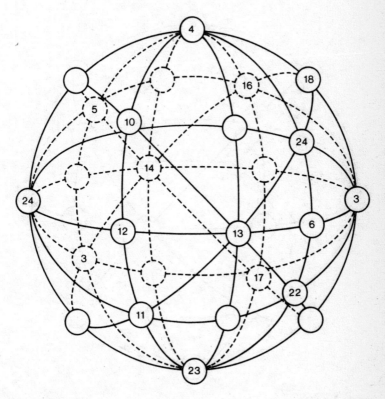

Puzzle No. 59

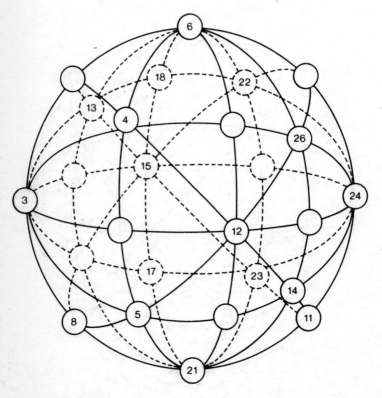

Puzzle No. 60

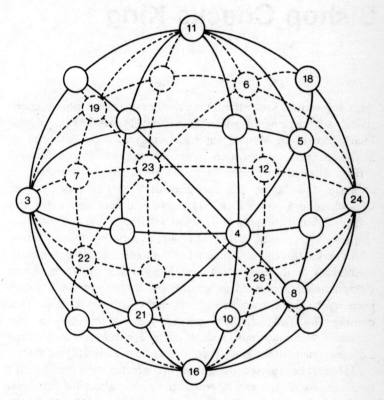

Puzzle No. 61

51

Chapter Fourteen

Bishop Checks King

'May I now draw your attention to this design carved into the choir-stalls,' said the cathedral guide. 'In mediaeval times the game of Nine Men's Morris, or Merels, was widely played. It is mentioned by Shakespeare in *A Midsummer Night's Dream,* and its popularity is further attested to by the fact that every English cathedral of monastic foundation has the grid of a merels board carved somewhere in its stonework or joinery. And here we see it in this cathedral; but if you look closely you will notice that at some of the corners and intersections the craftsman has carved certain numerals, which makes this carving unique. Legend has it that at the time of the dissolution of the monasteries in Henry VIII's reign, the Royal Commissioner appointed to arrange the transfer of the Church's property to the Crown lodged overnight with the Bishop. That evening the two of them played Nine Men's Morris, the Commissioner not winning a single game. The Bishop, who had been a student friend of the King, therefore wrote to Henry saying that he could hardly be expected to acquiesce in the forfeiture of the Church's land and revenue to someone who could not even beat him at Merels, and humbly petitioned the King for dispensation. Whereupon the King summoned the Bishop to Hampton Court and told him that the Church's lands would be forfeit in any case, but that if he could beat the King at Merels, the Bishop would be permitted to retain the teaching college attached to the cathedral.

'The King and the Bishop played for hours, first one gaining the advantage and then the other, but neither achieving the required margin for victory, till at last the King, his patience running out, said, "Prelate, we are clearly not destined to determine the issue in this fashion. Let us resolve it thus: let us both attempt to number each peg hole with a different number so that in every direction the lines joining them add up to the same total."

'The Bishop agreed, but with reluctance, for in their student days the King had surpassed all others in the subject of mathematics, a fact which the King was clearly hoping would be to his advantage. In the event, however, it was the Bishop's prayers which were answered, for he successfully solved the problem long before the King. To the King's credit he gave the Bishop dispensation in respect of the college which today still bears his name.

'Upon returning to the cathedral the Bishop instructed the master joiner to carve the numbers into the choir-stalls in thanksgiving to God — not all of them, but only these seven, to demonstrate, as he said, that it is not given to any man, not even a king, to know all there is about everything.

'Be that as it may, when this tour is completed I can be found in the local hostelry, in the friendly atmosphere of which I have sometimes been known to reveal the secret of the missing numbers to discerning tourists who appreciate the value of such esoteric knowledge.'

The grid of the merels board is shown below together with the seven numbers carved. Can you ascertain the missing numbers without having to buy the guide a pint? The constant you are seeking is 42, and the numbers are drawn from a broken series of 1 to 27. A further clue is that the constant is also produced by the four sections of the undrawn diagonals.

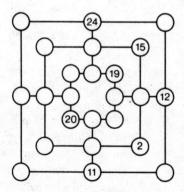

Puzzle No. 62

Four similar puzzles follow, all with a constant of 42.

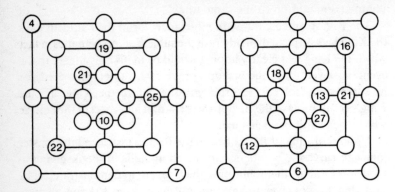

Puzzle No. 63

Puzzle No. 64

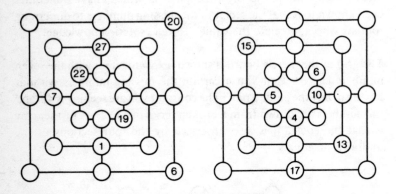

Puzzle No. 65

Puzzle No. 66

Chapter Fifteen

Miscellaneous Magic

Readers will have noticed from some of the previous chapters that magic squares can be formed into a wide variety of cross-sums, the process of extrapolation being more obvious in some of the shapes than in others. Here are a few more, all requiring completion to produce the respective constants.

Magic Honeycombs

In the following three puzzles the numbers 1 to 36 are so arranged in the cells of the honeycomb that the six numbers surrounding each black cell total exactly 111, even though some of the cells form part of two or three such groupings.

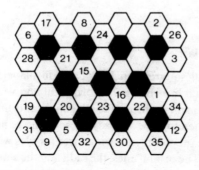

Puzzle No. 67

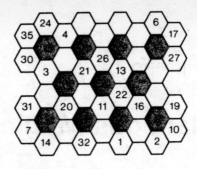

Puzzle No. 68

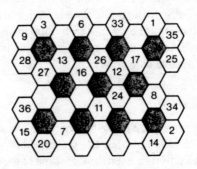

Puzzle No. 69

Magic Planetaria

All pandiagonal squares can be set out in planetarium form, the orbital and radial lines being the horizontal and vertical lines of the square, and the spirals being the diagonals and broken diagonals. They should therefore be as easy to solve as pandiagonal square puzzles, but are they? The following three puzzles will tell. The series used is 1 to 25. The orbital lines, the radii and the spirals all produce a constant of 65. One spiral is shown but there are of course ten – five in each direction.

56

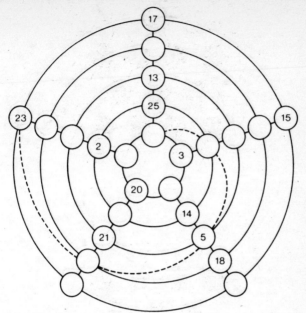

Puzzle No. 70

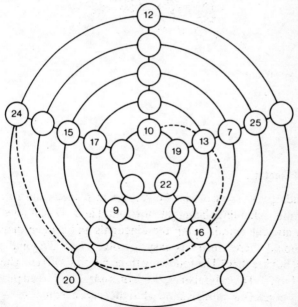

Puzzle No. 71

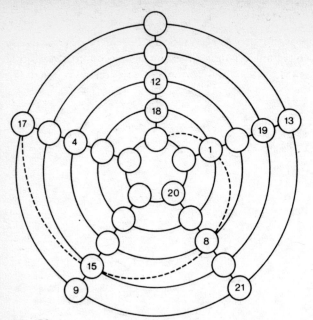

Puzzle No. 72

Magic Crystals

The following three puzzles are based upon magic crystals composed of seven rectangles, the corners of which are numbered from 1 to 16 in such a way that the four corners of each rectangle total 34.

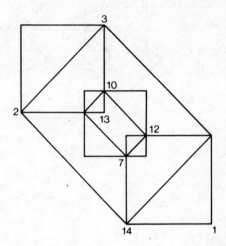

Puzzle No. 73

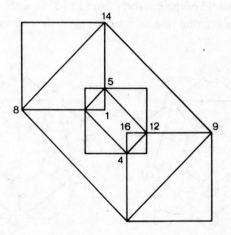

Puzzle No. 74

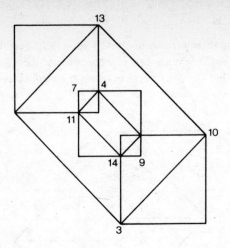

Puzzle No. 75

Magic Pentagons

The following three magic pentagons comprise eight separate pentagons sharing common sides and corners. The corners are numbered with 15 of the numbers from 1 to 25 in such a way that the five numbers surrounding each of the eight pentagons total 65.

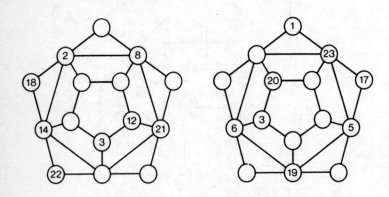

Puzzle No. 76   Puzzle No. 77

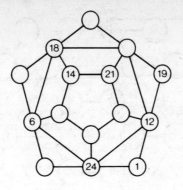

Puzzle No. 78

Magic Hexagons

In each of the following three magic hexagons there are nine separate hexagons, the points of which are numbered from 1 to 30 so that the six numbers surrounding each of the nine hexagons total 93.

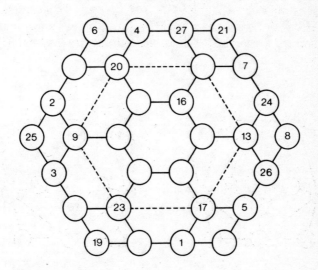

Puzzle No. 79

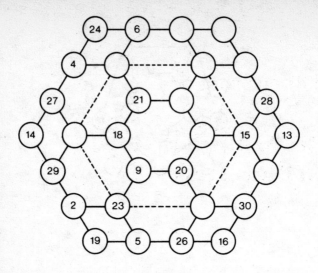

Puzzle No. 80

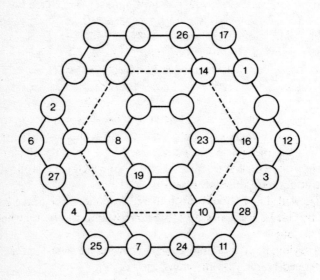

Puzzle No. 81

Chapter Sixteen

The Knight Errant's Further Task

Readers of *Number Puzzles* will doubtless remember the young knight errant who, in order to free the King's daughter imprisoned under a spell by the wicked Bandar, was set the task of traversing a chequered courtyard in chess-knight fashion. His success and valour were rewarded by the young maiden's hand in marriage, but the evil Bandar could not forgive him for frustrating his fiendish designs, and when in due course the young couple's union was blessed with the birth of a son, Bandar's rage knew no bounds. Seizing upon a moment when the infant was unguarded, Bandar plunged the babe into a stuporous slumber from which none could stir him.

'Well, young knight,' screamed Bandar, 'you thwarter of schemes! Let me see you lift this spell! The stakes are raised and the task more testing, for now, entering upon the courtyard here and moving only as a chess knight moves, you must number every square in turn so that the sum of every row, both north to south and east to west totals 260. Furthermore you must finish within a knight's move of the square from which you set forth, and from which I shall follow your frustration and failure with relish!'

''Tis well that I should finish there,' responded the brave knight, 'for, by Our Lady, I can scarce forbear to wait to cleave you when this task is done.'

So saying, he crossed himself and, drawing his sword in readiness, he stepped boldly into the courtyard.

To help you trace the young knight's steps, the fourth of all his moves is given, together with the additional information that each group of four moves occurred in the same quarter of the courtyard.

		49					
			13				
		33		17		21	
			61		45		9
1		37		53			
	29		25		41		
				5			
					57		

Puzzle No. 82

This knight's-move square is not a true magic square, since the diagonals do not produce the constant and cannot do so, one being wholly even and the other being wholly odd, an impossibility with true magic squares. In *Number Puzzles* I stated that I had been unable to devise more than four versions of the knight's-move puzzle, rotations and reflections excluded, but as this puzzle demonstrates, it is possible to increase the number considerably by dispensing with the requirement that each half row or column should total half the constant.

Four further puzzles follow, each requiring completion by numbered knight's moves to produce horizontal and vertical constants of 260. Again, every fourth move is provided as a clue.

Puzzle No. 83

			17				
		45					
			53		49		1
		41		13		29	
	21		5		33		
9		57		61			
					37		
				25			

Puzzle No. 84

					13		
				49			
	33		45		21		
61		17		9			
			1		25		53
		29		37		41	
			57				
		5					

Puzzle No. 85

			17				
		29					
			53		49		1
		25		61		13	
	21		5		33		
57		41		45			
					37		
				9			

Puzzle No. 85

Puzzle No. 86

					33		
				61			
	5		1		17		
57		29		45			
			37		21		49
		25		9		13	
			53				
		41					

Puzzle No. 86

Chapter Seventeen

Geometric Squares

The magic squares used so far in this book have been arithmetical squares, where the constant is produced by the addition of numbers in a particular group. It is no more difficult to create geometric magic squares where the constant is produced by multiplying the numbers together instead of adding them. Such geometric squares possess exactly the same characteristics as arithmetical squares. The same groupings produce the constant and pandiagonal geometric squares retain their magical qualities when columns and lines are transposed. The only difference between the two is the method of producing the constant – in one by addition, and in the other by multiplication. The constant, of course, is much larger with geometric squares, especially where the square includes no duplicated numbers, the lowest constant for such a four-power square being 5040.

The following five puzzles are all geometric squares, the first three of which contain some duplicated numbers. You are required to complete them to provide constants of 720, 2520, 2880, 5040 and 14,400 respectively. The last square is pandiagonal. Solving these puzzles should be no more difficult if you remember that the characteristics of geometric squares are exactly the same as those of arithmetical squares. The same lines, diagonals, quarters, corners and other groupings all produce the constant.

1	4		12
9			
		4	6

Puzzle No. 87

20			9
21			
	28	3	
			14

Puzzle No. 88

	2		
30			4
			6
1			20

Puzzle No. 89

		18	28
14			3
	4	7	

Puzzle No. 90

3			
			2
4			15
	60		

Puzzle No. 91

The expression of the large constants associated with geometric squares can be simplified by the use of exponents. The constant of the following geometric square, which numerically is over seventeen thousand million, can be expressed as 2^{34}.

2^5	2^3	2^{12}	2^{14}
2^{10}	2^{16}	2^7	2^1
2^{15}	2^9	2^2	2^8
2^4	2^6	2^{13}	2^{11}

The matter can be simplified further by reducing the exponents uniformly, thus creating negative powers. If those above were reduced, for example, by the power of 7, the result would be the following square with a constant of $2^6 = 64$.

2^{-2}	2^{-4}	2^5	2^7
2^3	2^9	2^0	2^{-6}
2^8	2^2	2^{-5}	2^1
2^{-3}	2^{-1}	2^6	2^4

You will no doubt have noticed that the exponents in the squares above themselves form a magic square, giving a clear indication of one of the methods by which geometric squares can be formed.

Chapter Eighteen

Magic Dominoes

A basic set of dominoes comprises 28 stones with spots ranging from 0–0 to 6–6. These stones can be laid out to form numerous magic rectangles in which the spots in the columns total 24, while the spots in the rows total 42. For example:

0-0	0-1	2-3	5-5	3-6	4-5	4-4
3-3	0-6	3-4	1-1	1-4	2-6	3-5
2-4	1-5	4-6	0-5	1-6	0-4	2-2
6-6	5-6	0-2	2-5	0-3	1-2	1-3

Since stones bearing the same number of spots are freely interchangeable, there are over one million ways of varying the rectangle above! There are, of course, many other basic layouts.

The magical potential of dominoes becomes more apparent, however, when three of the stones (0–5, 0–6 and 1–6) are discarded, for then the remaining stones can be laid out to form true five-power magic squares. The domino-square puzzles in this chapter are all pandiagonal. Ignoring reflections and rotations there are well over one million versions of such squares, but I trust that I will not be thought niggardly if I limit this chapter to just five of them! In solving these puzzles bear in mind that they conform to the rules for pandiagonal squares, namely that the broken diagonals and five adjacent squares in cross formation also produce the constant.

The solutions to the domino puzzles given at the end of the book are not unique. Because of the interchangeability of some stones there are alternative solutions.

The constant you are seeking is 30.

				0-0
3-5	0-2			4-5
		5-5		
		2-2	0-3	
2-3	0-4	4-4		

Puzzle No. 92

0-4		0-3		
	4-4		2-5	
	2-3			2-4
4-6	0-2	4-5		2-6

Puzzle No. 93

0-3		3-4		
2-6			2-2	
	2-3			
3-5				2-4
	5-5	0-2	4-5	

Puzzle No. 94

2-4		0-2		
		2-2	3-4	5-5
2-3				
		0-3		4-5
		4-6	3-5	

Puzzle No. 95

			2-5	
		3-6	2-6	0-2
4-6	1-3			2-4
2-3		4-4		
		0-3		

Puzzle No. 96

Chapter Nineteen

Three-dimensional Magic

It is possible to arrange consecutive numbers in the form of magic cubes in which the constant is produced not only across one plane but

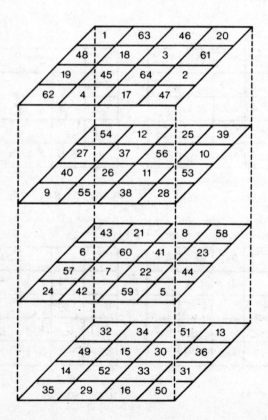

three-dimensionally through all planes. The magic cubes in *More Number Puzzles* contained 100 discrete groupings which produced the constant. This chapter explores their versatility a little further. Consider the magic cube opposite, each plane of which portrays a pandiagonal square.

In this cube the following groupings all produce the constant of 130.

	No. of groupings
the horizontal and vertical lines of each of the four grids	32
the vertical lines through all four grids	16
In the attitude depicted:	
the diagonals of each grid	8
the four corners of each grid	4
all groupings of four squares which form a square	36
the broken diagonals (4 × 6)	24
In the second attitude:	
six groupings of four squares which form a square in each grid	24
In the third attitude:	
seven groupings of four squares which form a square in each grid	28
the four corners of each grid	4
Making a total of	176

Although there are 176 groupings which produce the constant, some of them are not readily recognizable. It is, however, easy to solve the following puzzles by reference to the first six categories listed above, which comprise 120 groupings, without considering the others.

To make the matter of the three attitudes clear, when dice are thrown they can land with either the 1:6 axis, the 2:5 axis or the 3:4 axis perpendicular, so that the viewer can be presented with a cube in one of three possible attitudes. The magic cube set out above could be depicted as follows:

First, the original attitude:

1	63	46	20
48	18	3	61
19	45	64	2
62	4	17	47

54	12	25	39
27	37	56	10
40	26	11	53
9	55	38	28

43	21	8	58
6	60	41	23
57	7	22	44
24	42	59	5

32	34	51	13
49	15	30	36
14	52	33	31
35	29	16	50

Then, the first alternative attitude:

1	54	43	32
63	12	21	34
46	25	8	51
20	39	58	13

48	27	6	49
18	37	60	15
3	56	41	30
61	10	23	36

19	40	57	14
45	26	7	52
64	11	22	33
2	53	44	31

62	9	24	35
4	55	42	29
17	38	59	16
47	28	5	50

Last, the second alternative attitude:

1	48	19	62
54	27	40	9
43	6	57	24
32	49	14	35

63	18	45	4
12	37	26	55
21	60	7	42
34	15	52	29

46	3	64	17
25	56	11	38
8	41	22	59
51	30	33	16

20	61	2	47
39	10	53	28
58	23	44	5
13	36	31	50

From the diagrams above it is possible to see more easily the groupings in the alternative attitudes which produce the constant, but as was stated earlier, the following puzzles can be solved without considering these groupings if you wish.

In order to make the less obvious groupings clearer, the diagram opposite shows three characteristic groupings, marked A, B and C, each of which produces the constant, and shows in the attitude depicted groups of squares which in other attitudes will form one quarter of one grid. Provided one does not cross the boundary between quarters in any direction, one can choose any two pairs of squares sharing common sides and they will produce the constant.

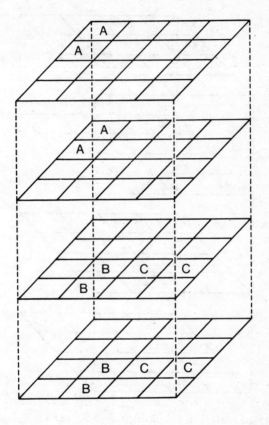

The ground-rules having been set out, the following four puzzles require completion to produce a constant of 130 in each case. Note that in these four puzzles the diagonals through the cube do not produce the constant, and that the grids are pandiagonal only in the attitude depicted. The puzzles can all be solved from the clues provided, without the need for trial and error.

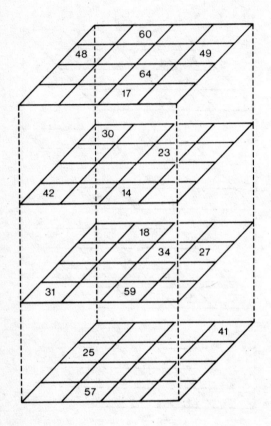

Puzzle No. 97

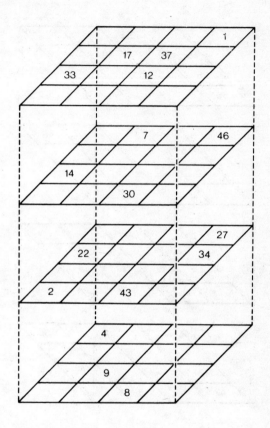

Puzzle No. 98

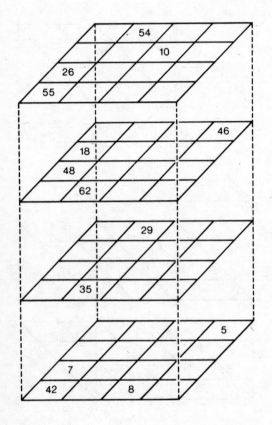

Puzzle No. 99

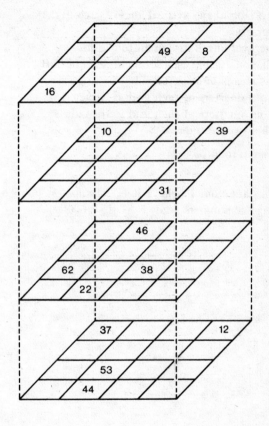

Puzzle No. 100

Finally, for readers anxious to test their pocket calculators to the full, a geometric magic cube!

The grids are not pandiagonal, so the groupings which produce the constant are:

	No. of groupings
the horizontal and vertical lines of each of the four grids	32
the vertical lines through all four grids	16
the diagonals from each corner of the cube (NB this means *through* the cube)	4
the four quarters of each grid as depicted	16
the four quarters of each grid in the cube's other two attitudes	32
Making a total of	100

The constant (and I believe it is the smallest possible without duplicating the numbers used) is 57, 153, 600!

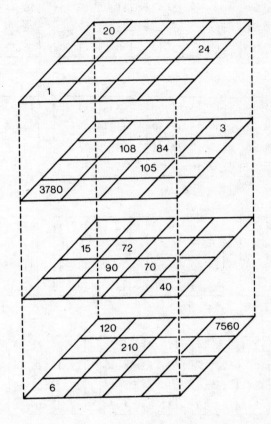

Puzzle No. 101

Solutions

100	140	150	110
190	70	60	180
80	200	170	50
130	90	120	160

1

4	15	10	5
6	9	16	3
13	2	7	12
11	8	1	14

2

17	16	12	5
11	6	18	15
14	19	7	10
8	9	13	20

3

21	27	12	18
16	14	25	23
26	20	19	13
15	17	22	24

4

21	30	23	16
15	24	29	22
28	19	18	25
26	17	20	27

5

12	13	1	8
6	3	15	10
7	2	14	11
9	16	4	5

6

8	1	13	12
11	14	2	7
10	15	3	6
5	4	16	9

7

11	13	8	2
4	6	15	9
5	3	10	16
14	12	1	7

8

1	15	8	10
4	14	5	11
13	3	12	6
16	2	9	7

9

4	6	11	13
9	15	2	8
14	12	5	3
7	1	16	10

10

12	17	16	5
15	6	11	18
9	20	13	8
14	7	10	19

11

13	3	6	12
8	10	15	1
11	5	4	14
2	16	9	7

12

12	15	9	14
17	6	20	7
16	11	13	10
5	18	8	19

13

10	23	16	21
24	13	18	15
19	14	25	12
17	20	11	22

14

20	26	21	23
29	15	28	18
24	22	25	19
17	27	16	30

15

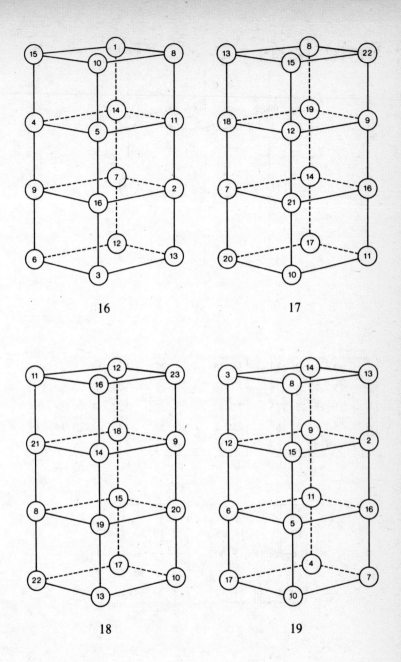

16

17

18

19

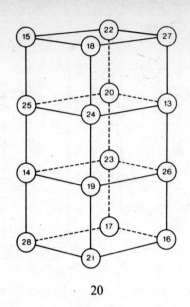

20

8	20	3	22	12
10	25	7	21	2
9	11	13	15	17
24	5	19	1	16
14	4	23	6	18

21

13	18	4	9	26
7	16	20	22	5
25	11	14	17	3
23	6	8	12	21
2	19	24	10	15

22

7	27	6	23	17
21	18	12	10	19
24	4	16	28	8
13	22	20	14	11
15	9	26	5	25

23

24	15	22	13	16
29	9	8	19	25
6	26	18	10	30
11	17	28	27	7
20	23	14	21	12

24

16	22	26	11	25
32	19	10	27	12
9	17	20	23	31
28	13	30	21	8
15	29	14	18	24

25

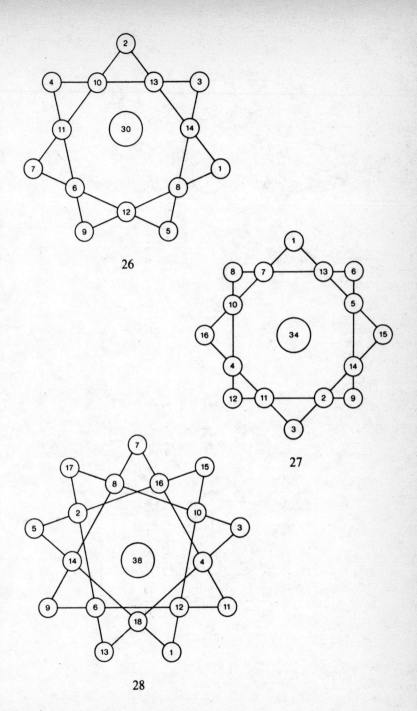

26

27

28

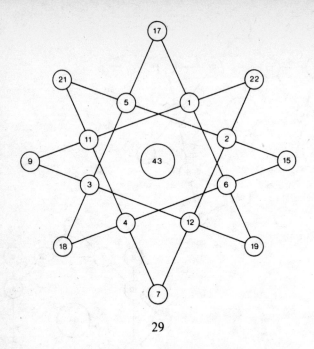

29

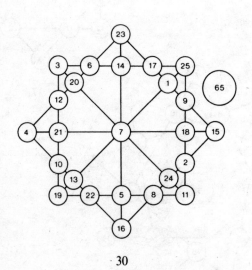

30

13	17	1	25	9
5	24	8	12	16
7	11	20	4	23
19	3	22	6	15
21	10	14	18	2

31

6	14	23	10	22
25	12	21	4	13
19	3	15	27	11
17	26	9	18	5
8	20	7	16	24

32

12	15	23	6	29
21	9	27	10	18
25	13	16	24	7
19	22	5	28	11
8	26	14	17	20

33

18	30	16	24	7
14	22	8	20	31
10	21	29	12	23
27	13	25	11	19
26	9	17	28	15

34

10	24	18	32	21
17	31	20	9	28
19	13	27	16	30
26	15	29	23	12
33	22	11	25	14

35

14	1	8	20	22
10	17	24	11	3
21	13	5	7	19
2	9	16	23	15
18	25	12	4	6

36

10	19	23	12	1
13	2	6	20	24
16	25	14	3	7
4	8	17	21	15
22	11	5	9	18

37

6	5	24	18	12
19	13	7	1	25
2	21	20	14	8
15	9	3	22	16
23	17	11	10	4

38

17	11	10	24	3
25	4	18	12	6
13	7	21	5	19
1	20	14	8	22
9	23	2	16	15

39

20	11	9	3	22
4	23	17	15	6
12	10	1	24	18
21	19	13	7	5
8	2	25	16	14

40

11	6	24	14	31	25
36	5	34	30	2	4
22	9	17	19	28	16
23	29	12	26	8	13
1	35	3	7	32	33
18	27	21	15	10	20

41

22	2	16	13	35	23
33	36	28	3	6	5
11	7	25	20	30	18
24	8	14	15	29	21
4	31	9	34	1	32
17	27	19	26	10	12

42

23	3	12	21	34	18
35	8	31	27	9	1
13	7	26	15	30	20
16	33	19	14	4	25
2	28	6	10	29	36
22	32	17	24	5	11

43

13	1	19	16	36	26
35	10	30	28	5	3
18	6	24	11	31	21
20	33	14	25	4	15
2	32	7	9	27	34
23	29	17	22	8	12

44

17	3	16	21	34	20
32	29	31	2	7	10
19	4	22	15	33	18
24	9	25	12	28	13
5	30	6	35	8	27
14	36	11	26	1	23

45

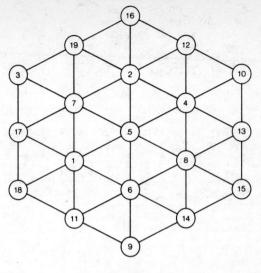

46

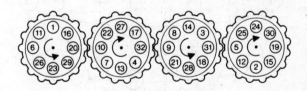

47

48

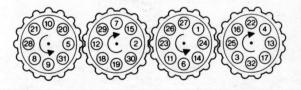

49

50

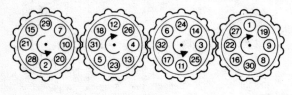

51

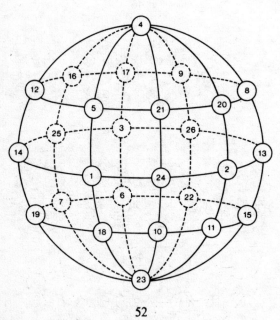

52

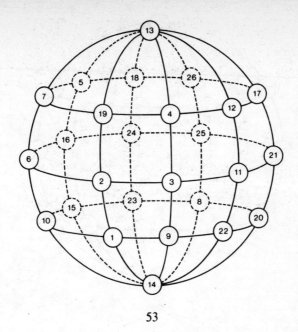

53

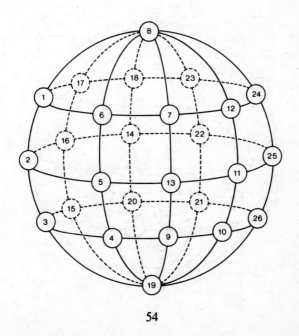

54

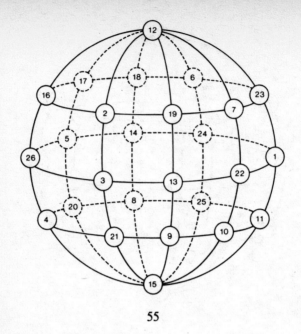

55

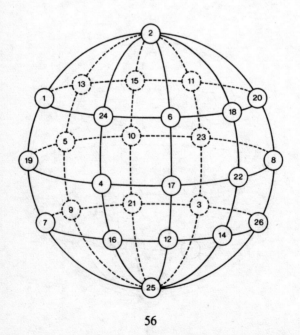

56

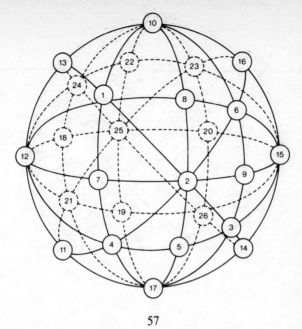

57

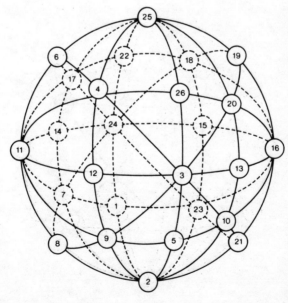

58

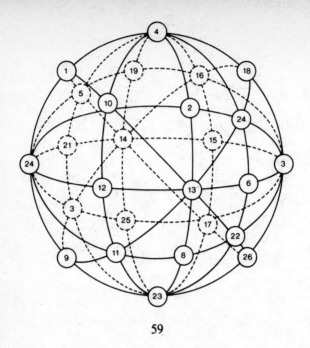

59

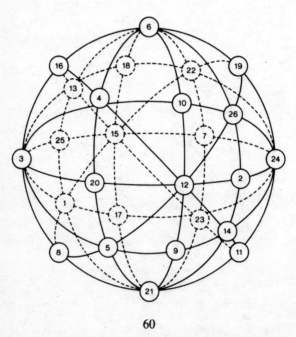

60

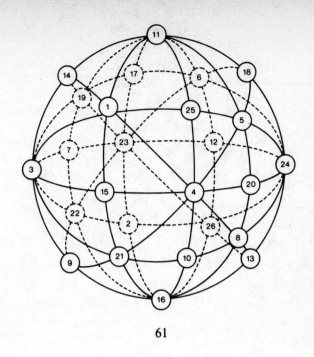

61

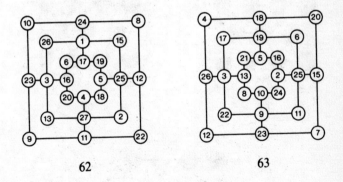

62   63

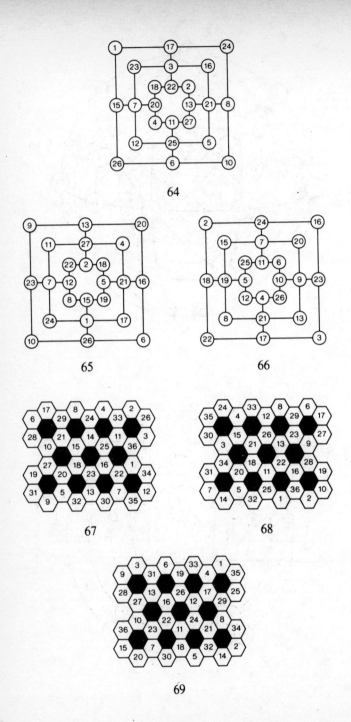

64

65

66

67

68

69

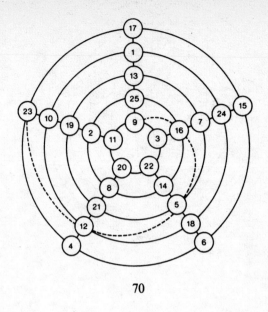

70

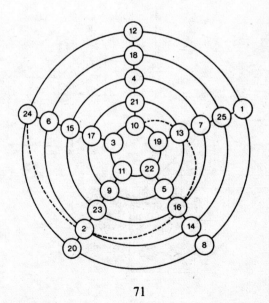

71

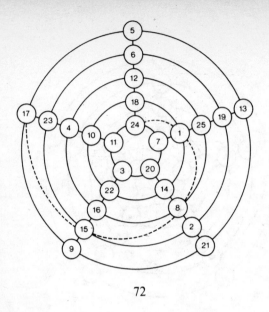

72

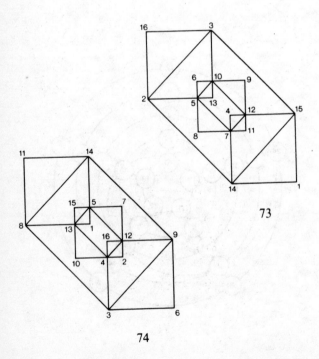

73

74

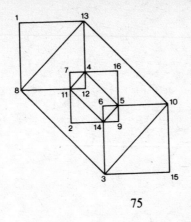

75

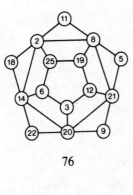

76

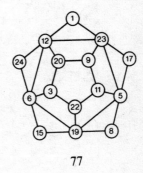

77

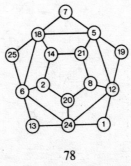

78

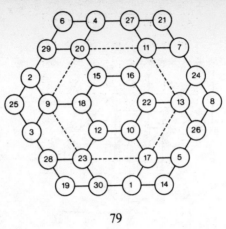

79

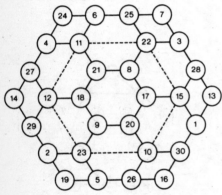

80

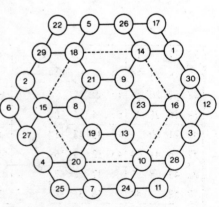

81

63	14	49	34	11	20	47	22
50	35	62	13	48	23	10	19
15	64	33	52	17	12	21	46
36	51	16	61	24	45	18	9
1	26	37	32	53	8	59	44
38	29	4	25	60	41	56	7
27	2	31	40	5	54	43	58
30	39	28	3	42	57	6	55

82

46	43	54	17	52	31	2	15
55	18	45	42	3	16	51	30
44	47	20	53	32	49	14	1
19	56	41	48	13	4	29	50
58	21	12	5	40	33	64	27
9	6	57	24	61	28	39	36
22	59	8	11	34	37	26	63
7	10	23	60	25	62	35	38

83

34	19	48	63	22	13	50	11
47	62	35	20	49	10	23	14
18	33	64	45	16	21	12	51
61	46	17	36	9	52	15	24
32	7	60	1	44	25	38	53
59	4	29	8	37	56	41	26
6	31	2	57	28	43	54	39
3	58	5	30	55	40	27	42

84

30	27	54	17	52	15	2	63
55	18	29	26	3	64	51	14
28	31	20	53	16	49	62	1
19	56	25	32	61	4	13	50
42	21	60	5	40	33	48	11
57	6	41	24	45	12	39	36
22	43	8	59	34	37	10	47
7	58	23	44	9	46	35	38

85

6	31	4	59	18	33	62	47
3	58	7	32	61	46	19	34
30	5	60	1	36	17	48	63
57	2	29	8	45	64	35	20
28	43	56	37	16	21	10	49
55	40	25	44	9	52	13	22
42	27	38	53	24	15	50	11
39	54	41	26	51	12	23	14

86

1	4	15	12
9	20	2	2
8	3	6	5
10	3	4	6

87

20	2	7	9
21	3	10	4
6	28	3	5
1	15	12	14

88

24	2	10	6
30	2	12	4
4	40	3	6
1	18	8	20

89

1	10	18	28
24	21	2	5
14	6	20	3
15	4	7	12

90

3	8	30	20
120	5	12	2
4	6	40	15
10	60	1	24

91

3-6	2-6	2-5	3-3	0-0
3-5	0-2	0-1	4-6	4-5
1-1	5-6	5-5	1-3	1-2
2-4	1-4	2-2	0-3	6-6
2-3	0-4	4-4	3-4	1-5

92

3-4	1-3	1-5	3-5	1-4
0-4	5-6	0-3	5-5	1-1
3-3	4-4	0-0	2-5	3-6
1-2	2-3	6-6	2-2	2-4
4-6	0-2	4-5	0-1	2-6

93

0-3	4-6	3-4	0-4	3-3
2-6	0-0	2-5	2-2	5-6
4-4	2-3	6-6	1-3	0-1
3-5	1-4	1-1	3-6	2-4
1-2	5-5	0-2	4-5	1-5

94

2-4	3-6	0-2	1-4	4-4
1-2	3-3	2-2	3-4	5-5
2-3	2-6	5-6	0-4	1-1
6-6	0-0	0-3	1-5	4-5
1-3	2-5	4-6	3-5	0-1

95

0-0	2-2	3-5	2-5	5-6
1-4	3-6	2-6	0-2	3-3
4-6	1-3	1-2	3-4	2-4
2-3	0-4	4-4	6-6	0-1
5-5	4-5	0-3	1-1	1-5

96

TOP

1	60	37	32
48	21	12	49
28	33	64	5
53	16	17	44

30	39	58	3
51	10	23	46
7	62	35	26
42	19	14	55

43	18	15	54
6	63	34	27
50	11	22	47
31	38	59	2

56	13	20	41
25	36	61	8
45	24	9	52
4	57	40	29

97

TOP

53	44	32	1
16	17	37	60
33	64	12	21
28	5	49	48

26	7	51	46
35	62	10	23
14	19	39	58
55	42	30	3

47	50	6	27
22	11	63	34
59	38	18	15
2	31	43	54

4	29	41	56
57	40	20	13
24	9	61	36
45	52	8	25

98

TOP

9	54	39	28
40	27	10	53
26	37	56	11
55	12	25	38

63	4	17	46
18	45	64	3
48	19	2	61
1	62	47	20

34	29	16	51
15	52	33	30
49	14	31	36
32	35	50	13

24	43	58	5
57	6	23	44
7	60	41	22
42	21	8	59

99

TOP

56	1	48	25
41	32	49	8
17	40	9	64
16	57	24	33

10	63	18	39
23	34	15	58
47	26	55	2
50	7	42	31

27	46	3	54
6	51	30	43
62	11	38	19
35	22	59	14

37	20	61	12
60	13	36	21
4	53	28	45
29	44	5	52

100

TOP

20	54	42	1260
1512	35	45	24
1890	28	36	30
1	1080	840	63

189	280	360	3
10	108	84	630
8	135	105	504
3780	14	18	60

126	420	540	2
15	72	56	945
12	90	70	756
2520	21	27	40

120	9	7	7560
252	210	270	4
315	168	216	5
6	180	140	378

101

Magic Square Puzzles

magic square compilation with 100 puzzles and solutions

Contents

Foreword

In preparing a book of puzzles based upon magic squares, it is necessary to begin by explaining the squares themselves; their basic principles, their different forms, and how they may be compiled.

I hope that this need is met in Part I. Doing homework on the subject of magic squares also reveals the difficulty of doing justice to the subsequent task of exposition.

Part II gives the puzzles and their solutions. Some puzzles may, perhaps, be solvable without reading Part I, but these will be a small minority.

The puzzles and solutions accord, generally but not essentially, with the methods and ideas of Part I – so that any puzzler is entitled (and welcome) to find valid solutions that differ from those given. Preferably, the given solutions stand, primarily, as proof of solvability. Many of the solutions are unique, of course.

With many of the solutions I include a note which seems relevant or helpful. However, I cannot believe that others would not find a note helpful in some cases where I see no great need for one!

As always, author and publisher have tried extremely hard to ensure that no errors slip by but, if they have, we will be grateful to hear of them.

PART I

Chapter One

Odd order squares

(e.g. 3×3, 5×5, etc)

The charm of magic squares is that they have little or no practical application that we can find. The ancient Chinese, however, produced as an amulet or talisman (hence 'magic') the Lo-Shu, whose modern form appears as Figure 1.1:

Figure 1.1

4	9	2
3	5	7
8	1	6

The Lo-Shu shows the principle of any magic, arithmetical, square; a square array of integers (whole numbers) such that the sum of the numbers in each row, column and corner-to-corner diagonal is the same (15, with the Lo-Shu). We will see that the numbers need not form a continuous series, neither need they start from 1.

A 3×3 square is called a third order square, 4×4 square is of the fourth order, and so on.

The other sort of magic square with which we will concern ourselves is the geometric square. We will see principles similar to those of the arithmetical squares, except that the numbers in each

3

line of the square multiply together to the same result rather than total (add together) to the same result. With geometric squares, we often find ourselves dealing with results that are staggeringly large, because as few as four or five small numbers, when multiplied together, can hardly show a modest result. We will deal later with geometric squares.

All normal magic squares show one only of each of their constituent numbers (cell values). Thus, a 5 × 5 magic square (for example) shows 25 different numbers. There are clear signposts when we depart (rarely) from this principle.

The Lo-Shu also shows other principles of regular odd order squares: the median, or middlemost, value always appears at the centre (well, almost always) and pairs of numbers (cell values) balanced about the centre show a common total (10, plainly).

Figure 1.2 shows, by two from several possible examples, that superficially different rearrangements of the Lo-Shu are possible merely by turning the square on its side. By reversing it; by turning it left to right, and so on.

Figure 1.2

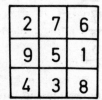 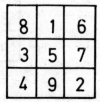

There are no fundamentally different arrangements possible with this basic third order square because, as a few trials can confirm, the centre cell must be occupied by 5 if a valid square is required.

Construction (regular arithmetical squares)

The common, easy, way of making all odd order squares was originated by a Frenchman, De La Loubère (1642–1729). His 'staircase' method can be understood from Figure 1.3 (a simple variation of the Lo-Shu) and an explanation follows. In passing, it's odd how certain seventeenth-century Frenchmen were fascinated by magic squares; the development of the subject came by their efforts.

Figure 1.3

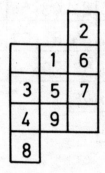

The first (lowest) number, or cell value, is placed in the centre cell of the top row. Sequent numbers are placed in diagonal progression upward to the right (a staircase). At the edge of the square, the next number is placed to complete its diagonal, if possible (as 3, in Figure 1.3). Otherwise, when meeting a filled cell or the edge of the square, drop to the cell next below and continue the staircase march on the new diagonal (as when 4 follows 3, in Figure 1.3). Thus, 7 is placed where shown after 4, 5, and 6 have been entered. Then, 8 and 9 complete the staircase diagram. Frankly, it's easier to do than to explain!

The magic square (see Figure 1.2 again) is made by putting 8 in the vacant corner cell above itself, and 2 in the vacant cell below itself. With familiarity, odd order squares can be compiled directly, using only a mental staircase.

We turn now to a fifth order square formed from the 25 numbers in the series: 7, 10, 13, 16 . . . 76, 79. According to principle, we start our diagonal march with 7 in the centre of the top row, which will allow us to end with a diagram looking like Figure 1.4.

5

Figure 1.4

				13
			10	31
		7	28	49
	19	25	46	52
16	22	43	64	70
34	40	61	67	
37	58	79		
55	76			
73				

By then entering the outside-square values in the empty cells, much as before, we have the completed square of Figure 1.5.

Figure 1.5

55	76	7	28	49
73	19	25	46	52
16	22	43	64	70
34	40	61	67	13
37	58	79	10	31

The total of the cells along any row, column and main diagonal (any 'line') of a magic square is called the magic constant of that square and, for regular squares, it is easily calculated. When 'n' is the order of the square: magic constant = (lowest cell value +

highest cell value) × n/2. With our fifth order square, the lowest value is 7, and the highest, 79: magic constant = (7 + 79) × 5/2 = 215. And, indeed, 215 is the total along any line of the square.

Because the cell pair totals in any regular odd order square are balanced about the centre cell, any of the 12 pairs gives the same result, e.g.:

(22 + 64) × 5/2 = 215
(37 + 49) × 5/2 = 215
(58 + 28) × 5/2 = 215.

Note, particularly, the concept of balance implied in the last pair, above. The cell values are, as the proper phrase has it, skewly related. The point is plain, from the figure.

Balance cell pairs are a feature of regularly constructed squares, whether of odd or even order, and such squares are often called 'associated' precisely because of the cell balance feature. All 'staircase' squares will be of associative form.

Note, also, the characteristic progression (increments) upward along the South West/North East main diagonal (SW/NE for future brevity): 37, 40, 43, 46, and 49.

A square generating series need not be continuous although, for De La Loubère, random, haphazard, numbers will not do. Figure 1.6 shows an array of dates from a calendar with, added for completeness, a few notional days at the month end. They form what we may call a discontinuous, although regular, series. The dates also may be regarded as 5 small, separate, series (each row), but the distinction is not important.

Figure 1.6

4	11	18	25	32
5	12	19	26	33
6	13	20	27	34
7	14	21	28	35
8	15	22	29	36

Our staircase starts with 4 at top row centre, of course, and Figure 1.7 shows the completed square with the outside-square staircase values marked for guidance.

Figure 1.7

14	29	4	19	34
22	32	12	27	7
25	5	20	35	15
33	13	28	8	18
6	21	36	11	26

The increment along the SW/NE diagonal is 7 (days in the week) as we might expect. The magic constant (100) may be found, as well, by using our formula and the highest and lowest cell values: $(4 + 36) \times 5/2 = 100$.

Only for odd order squares that will not lend themselves to the staircase method (e.g. squares to be formed from haphazard numbers) will we favour other ways. But there *are* other ways to form odd order squares from a regular series. Thus, using the same series that gave us Figure 1.7, we can have the square of Figure 1.8; one of countless possibilities.

Figure 1.8

4	13	19	28	36
26	35	8	11	20
15	18	27	33	7
34	5	14	22	25
21	29	32	6	12

Figure 1.8 is compiled by a method that we will explore in a later chapter – combining two Latin squares. The method has great value if we want to form squares, odd or even, from a random set of numbers. For now, we can note that the middle value of the series (20) is not at the centre of the square, as it will usually be, neither is there balance between cell value pairs; that is, the square is of neither regular nor associative form. But it is, nonetheless, a legitimate magic square. These sort of variations allow us to form some very complex puzzles.

However, Figure 1.8 shows a quality that does not arise naturally with our staircase construction method – the quality of pandiagonality. A pandiagonal square is one whose so-called broken diagonals also sum (in an arithmetical square) to the constant i.e., as well as the main, corner-to-corner diagonals. If we study again Figure 1.8, with reference to the position of the cells whose values now follow, we will see well enough what is meant by a broken diagonal and pandiagonality:

$$26 + 13 + 32 + 22 + 7 = 100$$
$$36 + 26 + 18 + 14 + 6 = 100$$
$$15 + 5 + 32 + 28 + 20 = 100$$

Plainly, there are many other examples within the same square.

Because an odd order square of associative form, such as that of Figure 1.7, is not naturally pandiagonal, it is safe to assume that everyone is dying to know how a conversion may be effected. Happily, it can be done without difficulty, certainly for fifth and seventh order squares although third order squares are among those orders for which pandiagonality is a technical impossibility with consecutive numbers. Note that, always, *all* broken diagonals must sum to the constant (multiply to, with a geometric square).

For a new basis of discussion, we will build a seventh order square starting at, say, 11 and proceeding by increments of 4 up to 203 as the highest cell value. Figure 1.9 shows the square with the residual staircase values marked merely for guidance.

Figure 1.9

127	163	199	11	47	83	119
159	195	35	43	79	115	123
191	31	39	75	111	147	155
27	63	71	107	143	151	187
59	67	103	139	175	183	23
91	99	135	171	179	19	55
95	131	167	203	15	51	87

We now re-draw our square, entering first a bottom row comprised of the cell value along the NW/SE diagonal of Figure 1.9. We then enter, as a top row, the cell values next below those same diagonal cell values of Figure 1.9. Which gives us, as a halfway stage, Figure 1.10. Note how the extreme right hand column is handled; because of the cyclic nature of magic squares. That is, any square may be regarded as part of an infinitely repeated pattern.

Figure 1.10

159	31	71	139	179	51	119
127	195	39	107	175	19	87

If we then complete each column, with its values in the same sequence as before, we have the seventh order pandiagonal magic square of Figure 1.11.

Figure 1.11

159	31	71	139	179	51	119
191	63	103	171	15	83	123
27	67	135	203	47	115	155
59	99	167	11	79	147	187
91	131	199	43	111	151	23
95	163	35	75	143	183	55
127	195	39	107	175	19	87

Conversion to pandiagonal form in this fashion destroys the pure associative form although, by other means, it is often possible to construct squares that are both pandiagonal and of the associative form. Different orders of square allow different forms of manipulation.

It is a remarkable feature of pandiagonal squares that if a square is (mentally) divided between any two rows or columns, the two pieces thus formed may be interchanged without disturbing the pandiagonality. Thus, with some orders of square (fifth and seventh, anyway, for our purposes) it is possible to restore the associative form to a square that has lost it. Figure 1.12 shows such a rearrangement of the rows of Figure 1.11 (interchange about the lateral marks).

11

Figure 1.12

59	99	167	11	79	147	187
91	131	199	43	111	151	23
95	163	35	75	143	183	55
127	195	39	107	175	19	87
159	31	71	139	179	51	119
191	63	103	171	15	83	123
27	67	135	203	47	115	155

We may calculate our constant as usual: $(11 + 203) \times 7/2 = 749$. And, checking a few broken diagonals from Figure 1.12:

$$191 + 31 + 39 + 75 + 111 + 147 + 155 = 749$$
$$91 + 99 + 135 + 171 + 179 + 19 + 55 = 749$$
$$27 + 99 + 199 + 75 + 175 + 51 + 123 = 749$$

For changing *from* pandiagonal form, the process is reversible.

Construction (regular geometric squares)

The simplest type of third order geometric square is based upon any 9 numbers in a geometric (instead of arithmetical) sequence. Thus, a series where each element is doubled would be the following: 1, 2, 4, 8, 16, 32, 64, 128, and 256.

The geometric square is formed in the usual staircase manner.

Figure 1.13

128	1	32
4	16	64
8	256	2

The magic geometric constant can be found by multiplying together the cell values in any line; the connection with arithmetical squares is obvious: $1 \times 16 \times 256 = 4096$; $128 \times 16 \times 2 = 4096$ (etc).

If we use n/2 as a power to be applied to the product of lowest and highest cell values (instead of, as with arithmetical squares, a factor to be applied to the sum of lowest and highest) we again find the constant: $(1 \times 256)^{3/2} = 4096$; $(4 \times 64)^{3/2} = 4096$ (etc.).

The calculation of powers (fractional, half, powers for odd orders) is unavoidable with geometric squares. Unless, of course, we multiply together all of the cell values in any line. But remember that a (say) 3/2 power is equal to the square root of a cube. A 5/2 power is merely the square root of a fifth power, and so on. Any of today's cheap electronic calculators will deal with the matter in very short order. The only real problem will be that of calculator capacity (magic geometric constants often need more than 8 digits).

A simple multiplication matrix (Table 1.1) will give us the basis for a fifth order geometric square based upon a discontinuous series. Much as when we used, earlier, handy dates from a calendar. Note the constant multiplication ratios (2, in one direction, and 3 in the other. Hence, a valid series).

	2	4	8	16	32	
1½	3	6	12	24	48	
4½	9	18	36	72	144	
13½	27	54	108	216	432	
40½	81	162	324	648	1296	
121½	243	486	972	1944	3888	Table 1.1

Figure 1.14 shows the resulting square, with outside-square staircase details marked for guidance.

Figure 1.14

162	1944	3	36	432
972	48	18	216	81
24	9	108	1296	486
144	54	648	243	12
27	324	3888	6	72

In accordance with the usual drill: constant $= (3 \times 3888)^{5/2} = 14,693,280,768$. Equally, if we multiply together a few cell values: constant $= 162 \times 48 \times 108 \times 243 \times 72 = 14,693,280,768$; constant $= 972 \times 48 \times 18 \times 216 \times 81 = 14,693,280,768$. As this is a regular, associated, square we still find balanced cell values. For example: $(1944 \times 6)^{5/2} = 14,693,280,768$; $(144 \times 81)^{5/2} = 14,693,280,768$. And, not surprisingly, we find geometrical (constant factor) progression upward along the SW/NE diagonal (2, with this example): $27 \times 54 \times 108 \times 216 \times 432 = 14,693,280,768$.

As with the arithmetical associative form squares, odd order geometric squares may be converted to pandiagonal form by the same manoeuvre: the NW/SE diagonal becomes a bottom row, and so on. Hence, Figure 1.15.

Figure 1.15

972	9	648	6	432
24	54	3888	36	81
144	324	3	216	486
27	1944	18	1296	12
162	48	108	243	72

A minute or two's work will show that the cell values along each of the broken diagonals multiply to the geometric constant, thereby proving pandiagonality in the square.

14

The square can have its associative quality restored by interchanging the upper and lower segments; marked at the side.

Let us close the chapter. and horrify ourselves, with a truly awful example of the square-maker's art. We will make a seventh order square from the multiplication matrix of Table 1.2:

	2	4	8	16	32	64	128
1½	3	6	12	24	48	96	192
4½	9	18	36	72	144	288	576
13½	27	54	108	216	432	864	1728
40½	81	162	324	648	1296	2592	5184
121½	243	486	972	1944	3888	7776	15552
364½	729	1458	2916	5832	11664	23328	46656
1093½	2187	4374	8748	17496	34992	69984	139968

Table 1.2

We might at once calculate the geometric constant: $(3 \times 139.968)^{7/2} = 4.7976111 \times 10^{19}$. This sort of scientific notation is the only way that most electronic calculators can show the result. For the full answer we must resort to more time consuming methods and find the following: 47,976,111,050,506,371,072. Some number! Never mind. Figure 1.16 shows the completed square.

Figure 1.16

486	5832	69984	3	36	432	5184
2916	34992	192	18	216	2592	243
17496	96	9	108	1296	15552	1458
48	576	54	648	7776	729	8748
288	27	324	3888	46656	4374	24
1728	162	1944	23328	2187	12	144
81	972	11664	139968	6	72	864

In deference to any scientifically minded readers, I must modify my earlier statement about the lack of practical use for magic squares. Most particularly, Latin squares (a form of magic square, of which more later) are an essential feature in statistical investigations of many kinds.

Chapter Two

Even order squares

(e.g. 4 × 4, 6 × 6, etc)

In Albrecht Dürer's famous engraving 'Melancholy' there is a modern (by comparison with the Lo-Shu of ancient China) example of a magic square (Figure 2.1).

Figure 2.1

16	3	2	13
5	10	11	8
9	6	7	12
4	15	14	1

The date of the work (1514) is seen in the two centre cells of the bottom row.

By using the lowest and highest cell values we may find the magic constant: $(1 + 16) \times 4/2 = 34$. The square is of the associative form, and cell pair values balance about the centre point – much as when there is cell value balance about the centre *cell* with odd order squares. Thus, each cell pair total equals 17, with the 'Melancholy' square; as they will with any magic square built upon a 1 to 16 series.

In dealing, next, with construction methods, we must treat separately the squares of doubly even order (divisible by both 4 and 2, e.g. 4, 8, 12) and those of singly even order (divisible by 2 only, e.g. 6, 10, 14).

Construction (regular arithmetical squares, doubly even)

We will find it convenient to adopt a construction method slightly different from that of the 'Melancholy' square.

Figure 2.2

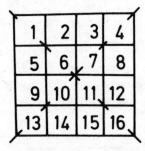

Figure 2.2 shows a 4 × 4 natural (seriatim) square with the main diagonal cells emphasised.

We now replace each value along each diagonal by its complement to 17 (the sum of cell pairs, of course). Thence, 16 will replace 1, 7 will replace 10, and so on. With any main diagonal, this is, in effect, a simple reversal of the run of the values (Figure 2.3).

Figure 2.3

16	2	3	13
5	11	10	8
9	7	6	12
4	14	15	1

We might expect that a discontinuous series would also generate a valid square. We again select from the calendar, reversing the rows to add a little variety (Figure 2.4).

Figure 2.4

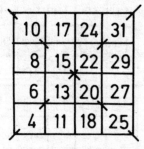

By reversing each diagonal, we have Figure 2.5.

Figure 2.5

25	17	24	4
8	20	13	29
6	22	15	27
31	11	18	10

From the lowest cell value (4) and the highest (31), we find the magic constant: $(4 + 31) \times 4/2 = 70$.

Notice that we still have progression along the SW/NE diagonal, although in reverse order, it happens, because we shuffled the originating series (though this is not important).

The next squares in the class of doubly even are those of the eighth order. We will use a natural (1 to 64) square to show that our same principles apply (Figure 2.6).

Figure 2.6

1	2	3	4	5	6	7	8
9	10	11	12	13	14	15	16
17	18	19	20	21	22	23	24
25	26	27	28	29	30	31	32
33	34	35	36	37	38	39	40
41	42	43	44	45	46	47	48
49	50	51	52	53	54	55	56
57	58	59	60	61	62	63	64

I have marked our 8 × 8 square with the main diagonals of each
of its 4 × 4 segments (quadrants). These diagonal cell values we
replace with their complements to 65; the balanced cell total that
applies to the full square, of course. Note that, with part (4 cell)
diagonals, this procedure is not the same as simply reversing the
run of the cell values (Figure 2.7).

Figure 2.7

64	2	3	61	60	6	7	57
9	55	54	12	13	51	50	16
17	47	46	20	21	43	42	24
40	26	27	37	36	30	31	33
32	34	35	29	28	38	39	25
41	23	22	44	45	19	18	48
49	15	14	52	53	11	10	56
8	58	59	5	4	62	63	1

The magic constant is, by the usual arithmetic, 260.

All squares built like this (doubly even, only) are of the associative form and can be easily converted to pandiagonal form if we first remember to mentally quarter any such square in the fashion shown by Figure 2.8.

Figure 2.8

Each quadrant of the square is treated as follows: A – remains unaltered; B – the columns are reversed, left to right; C – the rows are reversed, bottom to top; D – both columns and rows are reversed. This is the same as simply interchanging the two cell values of each balanced pair *position* within the quadrant. Actual pair values will not all balance, because the quadrant is not magic of itself.

With Figure 2.5 as a conversion example, this is the effect of the above changes (Figure 2.9).

Figure 2.9

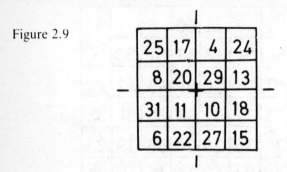

Figure 2.9 shows a perfect pandiagonal square lacking, as it must, associativity. With doubly even squares, pandiagonality and associativity can be combined only in orders above the fourth (i.e. 8, 12, etc.) but we won't explore this aspect of big squares.

If we apply our conversion method to the eighth order square of Figure 2.7, this is the result (Figure 2.10):

Figure 2.10

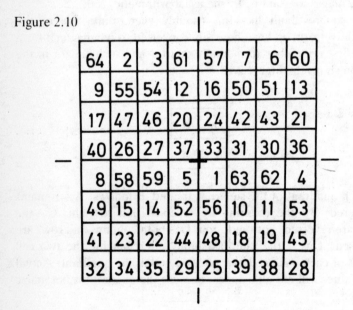

Construction (regular geometric squares, doubly even).

The simple multiplication matrix of Table 2.1 is the basis for a fourth order geometric square.

	½	1½	4½	13½
4	2	6	18	54
8	4	12	36	108
16	8	24	72	216
32	16	48	144	432

Table 2.1

Figure 2.11 shows the square (cell pair value 864) with each cell along the main diagonals replaced by the factor: 864/ cell value. Thus, 72 is replaced by 12 (i.e. 864/72) and so on. As with a fourth order arithmetical square, this is equivalent to reversing the run of cell values along the diagonals of Table 2.1.

Figure 2.11

432	6	18	16
4	72	24	108
8	36	12	216
54	48	144	2

The geometric constant is: $864^{+2} = 746496$ (i.e. 864^2).

As before, we may convert the square to pandiagonal form, using the ABCD quadrant of Figure 2.8 to make Figure 2.12.

Figure 2.12

432	6	16	18
4	72	108	24
54	48	2	144
8	36	216	12

23

Eighth order geometric squares can be formed in the way we know from working out eighth order arithmetical squares. Twelfth order, or higher order, squares can be formed similarly, but matters become a little unwieldy.

Construction (regular arithmetical squares, singly even)

Squares of the orders 6, 10, 14, and so on are acknowledged as offering the maximum resistance to easy construction methods. However, sixth order squares (non-associative, unavoidably) may be created by a scheme based upon that for doubly even squares. Figure 2.13 shows an orderly array that will suit our needs.

Figure 2.13

32	39	46	53	60	67
27	34	41	48	55	62
22	29	36	43	50	57
17	24	31	38	45	52
12	19	26	33	40	47
7	14	21	28	35	42

In the usual fashion, we will reverse the main diagonal cell values and, for a moment, ignore the letter notation (Figure 2.14).

Figure 2.14

42	a39	46	53	60	7
c27	40	41	b48	19	c62
22	29	38	31	50	e57
17	f24	43	36	f45	e52
12	55	26	b33	34	47
67	a14	d21	d28	35	32

As shown, the square of Figure 2.14 is not entirely magic. To achieve the desired effect, we will need to interchange similarly lettered cell values in each row or column. Which means that, for example, 39 changes with 14, and so on. The result is as Figure 2.15, a sixth order magic square, non-associated, but retaining diagonal progression.

Figure 2.15

42	14	46	53	60	7
62	40	41	33	19	27
22	29	38	31	50	52
17	45	43	36	24	57
12	55	26	48	34	47
67	39	28	21	35	32

The arithmetical constant is: $(7 + 67) \times 6/2 = 222$.

For another example of a sixth order arithmetical square, we take a simple arithmetical series, starting with 7 and proceeding by 35 increments of 3 to finish at 112 (Figure 2.16).

Figure 2.16

7	10	13	16	19	22
25	28	31	34	37	40
43	46	49	52	55	58
61	64	67	70	73	76
79	82	85	88	91	94
97	100	103	106	109	112

In Figure 2.17 we see the reversed main diagonals.

Figure 2.17

112	10	13	16	19	97
25	91	31	34	82	40
43	46	70	67	55	58
61	64	52	49	73	76
79	37	85	88	28	94
22	100	103	106	109	7

In Figure 2.18 we see our interchanged cell values (6 pairs, lettered 'a' to 'f' in Figure 2.14.

Figure 2.18

112	100	13	16	19	97
40	91	31	88	82	25
43	46	70	67	55	76
61	73	52	49	64	58
79	37	85	34	28	94
22	10	106	103	109	7

The arithmetical constant is: $(7 + 112) \times 6/2 = 357$.

Arithmetical and geometric magic squares of singly even order can be made pandiagonal or associative only with carefully contrived series and, even then, the construction methods make strong men weep. I propose to forget the whole idea and move to the matter of building basic magic squares of the tenth order. The method is, more or less, that of Ralph Strachey (circa 1918). All too often, the written explanation of a procedure imparts an aura of difficulty to that which is simple in practice and, sadly, what follows is no exception. We will use the natural 1 to 100 series of numbers.

First we see, in Figure 2.19, a basic fifth order magic square made by the staircase method. Later, it will be superimposed upon each of the four quadrants in a specially built 10×10 square.

Figure 2.19

17	24	1	8	15
23	5	7	14	16
4	6	13	20	22
10	12	19	21	3
11	18	25	2	9

27

Our next figure (Figure 2.20) shows a fifth order Latin diagonal square. We will be turning our attention to such squares in the next chapter but, for now, note that it is a simple matrix in which each symbol, or number, appears once only in each row, column and main corner-to-corner diagonal. For our present construction exercise, we will be using the Latin square only as an odd/even decision reference; but all will become plain.

Figure 2.20

4	1	3	5	2
3	5	2	4	1
2	4	1	3	5
1	3	5	2	4
5	2	4	1	3

Now, in the top left quadrant of Figure 2.21 we see an array of numbers 0 and 75. Valid arrangement possibilities are legion, but it is convenient to use our Latin square, replacing all the odd values by 75 and all the even values by 0. So that the top line of the quadrant is 0, 75, 75, 75, 0; corresponding to 4, 1, 3, 5, 2 in the top line of the Latin square. And so on.

The bottom left quadrant is a simple reversal of the top left quadrant, and with 0 replacing 75 (and vice versa) throughout. Thus, for example, the fourth row from the top, in the upper quadrant, is 75, 75, 75, 0, 0. The fourth row from the bottom, in the lower quadrant is 0, 0, 0, 75, 75. And so on.

In the top right quadrant, the top five ten-cell rows are each completed by whatever combination of cell values 25 and 50 will bring each full row to a total of 375 (explanation follows). Happily, the process is almost self-deciding.

Explanation: by usual arithmetic, the constant for the 1 to 100 square is 505 and, of course, the constant for the fifth order square (two of which will shortly be grafted onto the top half of the main square) is 65. Therefore, we calculate as follows to find the total for each row at this intermediate stage: 505 − (2 × 65) = 375. The top right quadrant can, as I suggest, be filled without too much bother, but remember that each main diagonal of the full square must also total to 375.

The bottom right quadrant is to the top right quadrant as the bottom left is to the top left; that is, a reversal of the sort already explained.

Figure 2.21

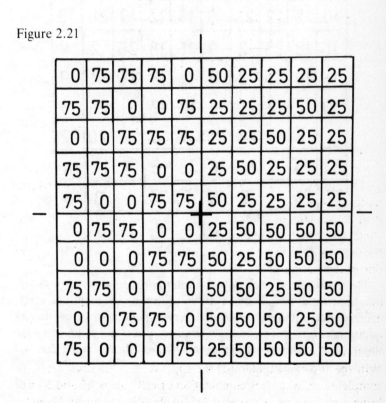

0	75	75	75	0	50	25	25	25	25
75	75	0	0	75	25	25	25	50	25
0	0	75	75	75	25	25	50	25	25
75	75	75	0	0	25	50	25	25	25
75	0	0	75	75	50	25	25	25	25
0	75	75	0	0	25	50	50	50	50
0	0	0	75	75	50	25	50	50	50
75	75	0	0	0	50	50	25	50	50
0	0	75	75	0	50	50	50	25	50
75	0	0	0	75	25	50	50	50	50

Each of the two upper quadrants of Figure 2.22 shows our fifth order magic square (as Figure 2.19). Each of the two lower quadrants shows a simple upside-down reversal of these.

Figure 2.22

17	24	1	8	15	17	24	1	8	15
23	5	7	14	16	23	5	7	14	16
4	6	13	20	22	4	6	13	20	22
10	12	19	21	3	10	12	19	21	3
11	18	25	2	9	11	18	25	2	9
11	18	25	2	9	11	18	25	2	9
10	12	19	21	3	10	12	19	21	3
4	6	13	20	22	4	6	13	20	22
23	5	7	14	16	23	5	7	14	16
17	24	1	8	15	17	24	1	8	15

At last! Each cell of Figure 2.23 shows the total of corresponding cells in Figure 2.21 and Figure 2.22 giving us, plainly, a tenth order magic square. Not associative or pandiagonal, as that is impossible with a consecutive number series and a tenth order square, but a jolly good square nonetheless. It's a shame that we also lose diagonal progression.

Figure 2.23

17	99	76	83	15	67	49	26	33	40
98	80	7	14	91	48	30	32	64	41
4	6	88	95	97	29	31	63	45	47
85	87	94	21	3	35	62	44	46	28
86	18	25	77	84	61	43	50	27	34
11	93	100	2	9	36	68	75	52	59
10	12	19	96	78	60	37	69	71	53
79	81	13	20	22	54	56	38	70	72
23	5	82	89	16	73	55	57	39	66
92	24	1	8	90	42	74	51	58	65

This method repays one's understanding of it; a little application will show that squares of many other orders can be built upon it and, certainly, there is no better way of building squares of singly even order other than the sixth.

Another, perhaps easier, example may be useful, so that we will compile a basic sixth order arithmetical square by using the same method (magic constant, 111).

Figure 2.24

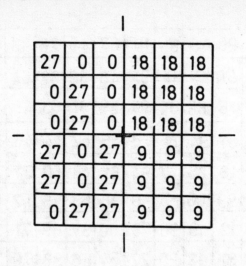

Figure 2.24 is, in principle, exactly as Figure 2.21 except only that, as a third order diagonal Latin square is a technical impossibility for a decision reference, we decide and place 0 and 27 (top left quadrant) directly at sight, and as may follow for the other quadrants. As the main square is not large (i.e. 6 × 6) any misjudgement is easily seen and corrected.

We will be superimposing on each quadrant a third order basic magic square (1 to 9, constant: 15) so that the total along each line of Figure 2.24 must be: 111 − (2 × 15) = 81.

Figure 2.25 shows our third order magic square placed (four times) and, in principle, it is exactly as Figure 2.22.

Figure 2.25

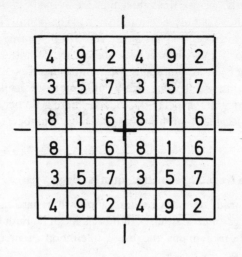

Figure 2.26 shows the finished square; each cell value being the total of corresponding cell values in Figure 2.24 and Figure 2.25.

Figure 2.26

31	9	2	22	27	20
3	32	7	21	23	25
8	28	6	26	19	24
35	1	33	17	10	15
30	5	34	12	14	16
4	36	29	13	18	11

There is a point about forming the initial quadrant squares, as in Figures 2.21 and 2.24. For the 1 to 100 square we used, 0, 25, 50, and 75 (pairing the two extremes with the two middlemost) and, for the 1 to 36 square, we used 0, 9, 18, and 27 (similarly paired). In other words, we use the values that are at the 0, 25th, 50th and 75th percentiles (as they say in statistics!). The point is that we are not absoutely obliged to start at the zero (0) percentile. We could have (say, for our sixth order square) 6, 15, 24 and 33 (suitably paired). When, at a later stage, we found ourselves adding (say) 33 to 8 for a final cell value, we would enter the result as 5 (i.e. $41 - 36$). Not a vital aspect and, indeed, there is no need to note it at all, but its mention hints at the huge number of possible variations.

Construction (regular geometric squares, singly even)

I propose to trade upon my readers' good will; regarding as proven the fact that geometric squares of this class can be built by familiar methods. There remains the usual likelihood of meeting some hefty numbers.

A point about pandiagonality. Remember that, when handling fifth and seventh order squares, interchanged parts of a pandiagonal square could restore to a square the lost quality of associativity. Unhappily, this wheeze cannot be made to work with even order squares. Indeed, of the even order with which we have dealt, it is only doubly even orders (4th, 8th, etc) that can be cast in pandiagonal form with any sort of ease. Other texts (see Appendix 2) explore these difficulties in greater detail.

Chapter Three

Latin squares

Our interest in Latin squares arises because, by their use, we can form magic squares of numbers in irregular or random series.

An ordinary Latin square can be defined as a square array of (typically but not essentially) integers, such that each integer appears once only in each row and column. If, also, each integer shows once only in each of the two main diagonals, the square is defined as a diagonal Latin square. Figure 2.20, earlier, is an example of a diagonal Latin square of the fifth order.

We concern ourselves only with diagonal Latin squares because they most readily lend themselves to our interests, but there are sometimes other Latin square routes to valid solutions.

Some principles outlined

A Frenchman, Phillipe de la Hire (1640–1718), is commonly credited with first using the method of adding, cell for cell, two Latin squares (not necessarily diagonal) to form a magic square. Our procedure is somewhat similar to this.

We will, therefore, need two diagonal Latin squares and, as our first example concerns a simple fourth order arithmetical (1 to 16) magic square, the fourth order diagonal Latin squares of Figure 3.1 (a) and (b) will suit very well. We will use them shortly. Technically, the squares form an *orthogonal pair* because, if superimposed, every cell value of one square matches once, and once only, with every cell value of the other square (more later!).

Figure 3.1

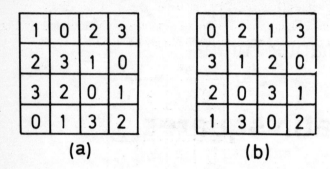

1	0	2	3
2	3	1	0
3	2	0	1
0	1	3	2

(a)

0	2	1	3
3	1	2	0
2	0	3	1
1	3	0	2

(b)

In Figure 3.2 we see a simple addition table, clearly designed to show the integers 1 to 16 by using the addition elements 0, 4, 8 and 12 with 1, 2, 3 and 4. We know, of course, that we could easily form a magic square by merely reversing the main diagonals, but we need an example upon which to build our methods of handling irregular numbers.

Figure 3.2

	1	5	9	13
1	1	5	9	13
2	2	6	10	14
3	3	7	11	15
4	4	8	12	16

0   4   8   12

By substituting the elements of Figure 3.2 for the cell values of Figure 3.1 (a) and (b) we compile, shortly, Figure 3.3 (a) and (b). There are heaps of substitution possibilities, but the following scheme serves:

	(a)	(b)
Cell values (Figure 3.1):	0 1 2 3	0 1 2 3
Cell values (Figure 3.3):	4 0 8 12	4 1 2 3

Thus, Figure 3.3 (a) shows 12 in each of the four cells of Figure 3.1 (a) that shows 3; correspondingly elsewhere.

Figure 3.3

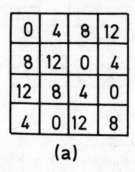

(a)

(b)   **(c)**

By adding (a) to (b), cell for cell, we derive (c), the magic square. It lacks subsidiary qualities (associativity and pandiagonality) but this may be expected with a construction method suitable for irregular numbers.

With equal validity, we might prefer to substitute on the following plan:

	(a)	(b)
Cell values (Figure 3.1):	0 1 2 3	0 1 2 3
Cell values (Figure 3.4):	12 0 4 8	1 4 3 2

This gives us Figure 3.4 (a) and (b) with, by cell for cell addition, the magic square of Figure 3.4 (c).

Figure 3.4

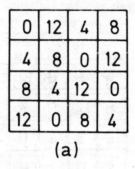

(a)

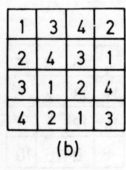

(b)

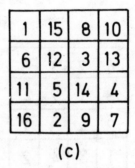

(c)

The astute reader will have realised that, for any arithmetical magic square, the magic constant is the sum of the addition elements. We may rightly infer that the *product of factors* will provide the constant in a geometric square.

Plainly, we are going to take these matters further but, for now, it seems best to look at methods of building Latin squares.

Construction (odd orders)

Only modest effort is needed to prove that there are no diagonal Latin squares of the third order. Which brings us to the fifth order of squares.

38

Figure 3.5 shows an ordinary addition table. In principle, much as we saw earlier, although we will find that its purpose is different. The addition elements show increments of 3 and 1 from convenient starting points of 0 and 1.

Figure 3.5

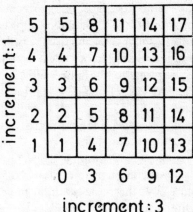

We next divide each cell value by 5 (the order of the square) and show only the remainder after such division in corresponding cells in Figure 3.6. For example, the top right hand cell of Figure 3.5 shows 17 but, after division by 5, we see the remainder (2) entered in the matching cell of Figure 3.6. The result is a fifth order diagonal Latin square.

Figure 3.6

0	3	1	4	2
4	2	0	3	1
3	1	4	2	0
2	0	3	1	4
1	4	2	0	3

It hardly matters but, technically, Figure 3.6 is a simple addition table of modulo 5.

With this example, we see that the required Latin square could be formed by cyclic permutation of the rows (or columns, for that matter) because each row has the same digit (cell) sequence. We won't find this possible with all orders of diagonal Latin square; only with all *prime* orders of square (5th, 7th, 11th etc.).

For any addition table (as Figure 3.5) to generate a diagonal Latin square, there must be certain relationships between the two addition increments (a and b, say) and 'n', the order of the square. With parenthetic notes relating to our latest example:

both a and b must be prime to 'n' (both 3 and 1 are prime to 5);

$a + b$ must be prime to 'n' (3 + 1 (i.e. 4) is prime to 5);

$a - b$ must be prime to 'n' (3 − 1 (i.e. 2) is prime to 5).

Numbers are prime to each other (i.e. relatively prime) if they have no common factor except 1.

For another example we will compile a seventh order diagonal Latin square, using the addition increments 3 and 5 (which satisfies the criteria). Figure 3.7, the basic addition table, shows that it doesn't much matter what starting numbers we use. Small numbers may save both time and ink.

Figure 3.7

increment: 3							
24	34	39	44	49	54	59	64
21	31	36	41	46	51	56	61
18	28	33	38	43	48	53	58
15	25	30	35	40	45	50	55
12	22	27	32	37	42	47	52
9	19	24	29	34	39	44	49
6	16	21	26	31	36	41	46
	10	15	20	25	30	35	40

increment: 5

After dividing each cell value by 7, the remainder is again entered into corresponding cells. The outcome is the seventh order diagonal Latin square of Figure 3.8:

Figure 3.8

6	4	2	0	5	3	1
3	1	6	4	2	0	5
0	5	3	1	6	4	2
4	2	0	5	3	1	6
1	6	4	2	0	5	3
5	3	1	6	4	2	0
2	0	5	3	1	6	4

Construction (even orders)

Diagonal Latin squares of the fourth order can be written almost at sight or, certainly, with very little further effort if the first trial or two shows an invalid square. Unhappily, that is as far as we can go with even order diagonal squares. The criteria that guided us when we compiled addition tables for odd order squares (Figures 3.5 and 3.7) cannot be satisfied when even orders of square are wanted. Which is not to say that such squares do not exist. The problem is one of construction; the only available methods require a fair degree of devotion to mathematical duty and are, therefore, unsuitable for us here.

Appendix 1 gives examples of diagonal Latin squares of all orders from four to eight; in fact, an orthogonal pair for each order is shown (except the sixth, about which there is comment shortly.)

Magic Squares (1)

We return to our main theme, building magic squares for almost any array of numbers, with an example whose construction will show us a pitfall whose future avoidance merits our vigilance.

Assume that we want to build a fourth order arithmetical square from these eight numbers:

3, 7, 12, 4, 6, 21, 5, 39 (total 97, the constant)

We know that these numbers (the addition elements) will be arranged into two fourth order diagonal Latin squares as a prelude to cell for cell addition. However, rather than go straight away to the substitution drill, it is always wise to first form an addition table (multiplication table, with geometric squares) to check for cell value duplication.

Superficially, it doesn't matter how we select our two groups of four from the eight available. Here are three ways from thousands (Figure 3.9):

Figure 3.9

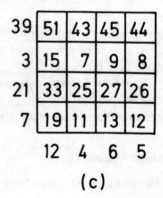

	9	24	8	42
3				
7	13	28	12	46
12	18	33	17	51
4	10	25	9	43

6   21   5   39

(a)

	51	45	60	44
39				
3	15	9	24	8
7	19	13	28	12
4	16	10	25	9

12   6   21   5

(b)

	51	43	45	44
39				
3	15	7	9	8
21	33	25	27	26
7	19	11	13	12

12   4   6   5

(c)

42

We see at once (cell values 9, in (a) and (b)) that only the grouping shown in (c) causes no cell value duplication. The interested reader can prove for himself that cell value duplication carries through to spoil the final magic square. A not-so-magic square, perhaps.

Within each group of four elements, it doesn't matter how we shuffle around; 3, 21, 39, 7, is as good as 39, 3, 21, 7. Duplication occurs when numbers are in the wrong group. More specifically, it occurs with matching differences, or increments, between any two elements in each group. With geometric squares, a matching *ratio* represents the pothole that upsets the apple cart.

With our present example, Figure 3.9 (a) and (b) are failures because the difference between 3 and 4, in one group, is the same as the difference between 5 and 6, in the other. However, we will use again the squares of Figure 3.1 in a substitution scheme having the addition groups of Figure 3.9 (c); the result, Figure 3.10, appears afterwards:

		(a)				(b)		
Cell values (Figure 3.1):	0	1	2	3	0	1	2	3
Cell values (Figure 3.10):	7	39	3	21	5	12	4	6

Figure 3.10

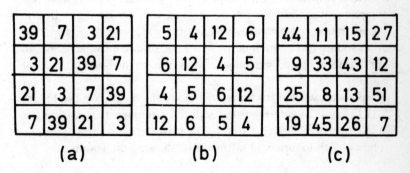

(a) **(b)** **(c)**

As usual, cell for cell addition shows the desired magic square in Figure 3.10 (c). Magic constant, 97, of course.

43

Next – another potential pitfall. There is also need for great care at the early stage of compiling the two diagonal Latin squares. It is only too possible to form two squares that are not complementary for our purposes. Refer to Figure 3.11 (a) and (b):

Figure 3.11

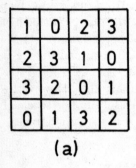

(a)

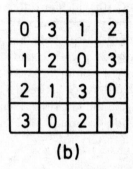

(b)

Figure 3.11 (b) is not complementary to (a) because, for example, each of its four digits 0 matches cell position with digit 1 in (a). Correspondingly with digits 1, 2, and 3. Everything matches. It would be impossible to have two squares that were less complementary for our needs. If even two similar digits in one square match cell positions with any two other similar digits in the other square (let alone four, as here) one square must be recast. In our earlier phrase, we must always use an orthogonal pair of squares.

However, we will continue; just to see the result. We use Figure 3.11 (a) and (b) with the same addition groupings that gave us the magic square of Figure 3.10 (c). The substitution scheme is as now follows, with Figure 3.12, afterwards, showing the results:

	(a)				(b)			
Cell values (Figure 3.11):	0	1	2	3	0	1	2	3
Cell values (Figure 3.12):	7	39	3	21	5	12	4	6

Figure 3.12

39	7	3	21
3	21	39	7
21	3	7	39
7	39	21	3

(a)

5	6	12	4
12	4	5	6
4	12	6	5
6	5	4	12

(b)

44	13	15	25
15	25	44	13
25	15	13	44
13	44	25	15

(c)

The magic square of Figure 3.12 (c) is magic, certainly, in the sense that it necessarily shows the constant of 97 but, essentially, we have another diagonal Latin square. The usual result of inadvertently adding values from two non-orthogonal squares is a defect hard to spot. Eyesight can play odd tricks when scanning for duplicated cells.

The fact that individual cell values will necessarily match cell positions *once* with orthogonal mates is unimportant. In Figure 3.1 (a) and (b) we see one for one cell position matching in the entire right hand columns of each square. As we know, this didn't upset our eventual magic square. Examples in Appendix 1 illustrate the point amply.

Magic squares (2).

Some further foundations of construction may be laid by seeing the working of specific problems without, now, totally concerning ourselves with the possibility of hideous blunder.

Problem 1: build a fifth order arithmetical magic square with a constant of 1066.

Solution: first, we set down any array of ten numbers that totals to 1066:

50, 7, 2, 11, 221, 42, 319, 70, 112, and 232

In Figure 3.13 we have the addition table to check for duplication:

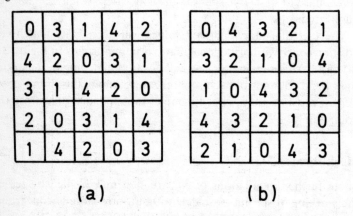

Figure 3.13

50	92	369	120	162	282
7	49	326	77	119	239
2	44	321	72	114	234
11	53	330	81	123	243
221	263	540	291	333	453
	42	319	70	112	232

There is no duplication and, as a check on arithmetic, we find that the total of all the cell values is 5330 (i.e. 5 × 1066) as it should be.

Figure 3.14

0	3	1	4	2
4	2	0	3	1
3	1	4	2	0
2	0	3	1	4
1	4	2	0	3

(a)

0	4	3	2	1
3	2	1	0	4
1	0	4	3	2
4	3	2	1	0
2	1	0	4	3

(b)

In Figure 3.14 (a) we have a fifth order diagonal Latin square (actually, a repetition of Figure 3.6). To form an orthogonal mate (Figure 3.14 (b)) we favour the useful ploy of reversing the run of the cell values along the north-south and east-west diagonals in (a). For example, 2, 1, 0, 4, in (a) becomes 4, 0, 1, 2, in (b). An orthogonal mate can also be found, often, by turning a square (in effect) through one or two right angles.

46

The following substitution scheme, used with Figure 3.14 (a) and (b), gives the result shown in Figure 3.15 (a) and (b) with, of course, (c) as the desired magic square, formed by cell for cell addition:

	(a)	(b)
Cell values (Figure 3.14):	0 1 2 3 4	0 1 2 3 4
Cell values (Figure 3.15):	50 7 2 11 221	42 319 70 112 232

Figure 3.15

50	11	7	221	2
221	2	50	11	7
11	7	221	2	50
2	50	11	7	221
7	221	2	50	11

(a)

42	232	112	70	319
112	70	319	42	232
319	42	232	112	70
232	112	70	319	42
70	319	42	232	112

(b)

92	243	119	291	321
333	72	369	53	239
330	49	453	114	120
234	162	81	326	263
77	540	44	282	123

(c)

(The next poser comes from reading, in the back of a reference atlas, that the population of the United States of America is 215,800,000; a good, useful, number.) So, *Problem 2:* compile a fourth order geometric square of constant 215,800,000.

Solution: by prime factorisation we reach the following from among many valid possibilities for eight factors: $2 \times 4 \times 8 \times 25 \times 25 \times 13 \times 83 \times 5 = 215,800,000$. In Figure 3.16 we have a multiplication table that confirms the absence of cell value duplication:

Figure 3.16

2	50	26	166	10
4	100	52	332	20
8	200	104	664	40
25	625	325	2075	125
	25	13	83	5

As a check on the working, the product of all the table values equals, as it should, the fourth power of the constant: $215,800,000^4 = 2.1687313697296 \times 10^{33}$ (exactly). Interesting, how results can run out a little on the big side.

As we have fourth order orthogonal mates in Figure 3.1 we will use them again:

		(a)					(b)		
Cell values (Figure 3.1):	0	1	2	3		0	1	2	3
Cell values (Figure 3.17):	2	4	8	25		25	13	83	5

As usual, the magic square appears in (c).

Figure 3.17

4	2	8	25
8	25	4	2
25	8	2	4
2	4	25	8

(a)

25	83	13	5
5	13	83	25
83	25	5	13
13	5	25	83

(b)

100	166	104	125
40	325	332	50
2075	200	10	52
26	20	625	664

(c)

To digress for a moment: there is a classic problem first put by the famous Swiss mathematician, Leonhard Euler (1707–83) about arranging 36 army officers, taken from six different regiments and of six different ranks. Each row and column of a 6 × 6 square was to contain only one officer of each regiment and only one officer of each rank. A solution to the problem would require that there are two ordinary (not diagonal) Latin squares of the sixth order that form an orthogonal pair.

It was shown, long ago, that no such sixth order pair can exist. That is, a sixth order Eulerian square (as it is called) is a practical impossibility. So that Euler's problem is insoluble. Our problem, consequently, is that there are severe limits to what we can do with related sixth order posers. It isn't hard to find oneself unwittingly trying to unscrew the inscrutable.

Eulerian squares are problems in arrangement rather than arithmetic, as we can see. For an easier proposition, there is another classic problem, with playing cards, that requires us to arrange the ace, king, queen and jack of each suit (16 cards in all) so that each full line (i.e. including the main diagonals) of a 4 × 4 square shows each rank once only and each suit once only. For a solution, we form a fourth order diagonal Eulerian square which, for patient readers who have come this far with me, should offer very few difficulties.

Empirical constructions

Although they are more time consuming than the addition table approach, largely empirical construction methods (trial and error, say) can produce diagonal (or other) Latin squares of all orders.

As a broad approach, used for one or two of the following puzzles, I find that a useful way is to first enter the top two or three rows as fancy may suggest, and then to settle the two main diagonals in the light of the constraints that will then exist. At least, the method seems to easily highlight any invalid start that may have been made. I make no great claims, though. The resulting squares offer the randomness that is denied one when using addition table schemes.

For a rough rule of thumb, I assume that the time taken to produce, empirically, a diagonal Latin square increases directly with the cube of the number of cells. Therefore, a sixth order square will take about eleven times as long to build as will a fourth order square (i.e. $36^3/16^3$). Clearly, one quickly reaches the point where Latin square empirical construction is abandoned in favour of canasta. Fairly typically, I think, a seventh order diagonal Latin square took me twenty-two minutes to construct with the above method.

PART II

Puzzle 1

Place the numbers 3 to 11 (both inclusive) so that the total is 21 in each row, column and both diagonals. The number 7 will be central, as shown.

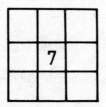

Puzzle 2

Place the nine numbers 10 to 18 (both inclusive) so that the total is 42 in each row, column and both diagonals.

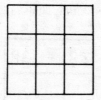

Puzzle 3

Place four even numbers so that the total is 45 in each row, column and both diagonals.

	3	
9	15	21
	27	

Puzzle 4

Place four odd numbers so that the total is 48 in each row, column and both diagonals.

	4	
10	16	22
	28	

Puzzle 5

The following numbers can be placed to show the same total in each row, column and both diagonals: 13, 23, 33, 43, and 53.

48		38
28		18

Puzzle 6

Place the following nine numbers so that the product (multiply together) is 13,824 in each row, column and both diagonals: 1½, 3, 6, 12, 24, 48, 96, 192, and 384.

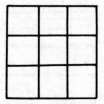

Puzzle 7

Place the following nine numbers so that the total is 99 in each row, column and both diagonals: 22, 23, 24, 32, 33, 34, 42, 43, and 44.

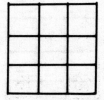

Puzzle 8

The diagram shows three numbers (correctly placed) from a series of nine consecutive numbers. The full series, when correctly placed, will show the same total in each row, column and both diagonals.

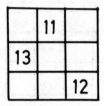

Puzzle 9

The diagram shows the position of the lowest number in the following series: 1, 2, 3, 4, 6, 9, 12, 18, and 36.

When the series is correctly placed in the square, the product (multiply together) in each row, column and main diagonal will be 216.

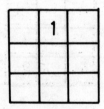

Puzzle 10

The largest of the numbers needed to fill the square is shown in its right place. The missing eight numbers are all prime, and the total along each line (the magic constant), when they are found and placed, will be 219.

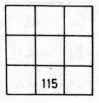

Puzzle 11

Each dot represents the same, missing, unit's digit. Thus, for example, the centre value cell might be (but isn't) 52. When found and placed, the square will show a constant of 171. The square is arithmetical.

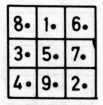

Puzzle 12

Each dot represents a missing unit's digit, either 3 or 8. Thus, for example, the centre cell value will be either 33 or 38. When found and entered in the (arithmetical) square, the magic constant will be seen as 114. No cell value is duplicated.

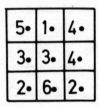

Puzzle 13

The diagram shows the correct position of the lowest number in a regular series that might begin (but doesn't): 19, 23, 27, 31, ...
   When the series is found, the diagram can be completed to show an arithmetical square with a magic constant of 141.

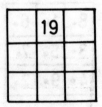

Puzzle 14

By adding to each cell value (correctly placed) in the left hand square, a value from a (non-corresponding) cell in the right hand square, a conventional arithmetical square can be shown. For example: (28+14) + (11+20) + (2+30) = 105.

Unhappily, though, the magic constant is not 105, so that further work will be needed.

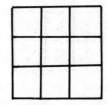

Puzzle 15

The cell values in the left-hand square are properly placed, but each needs augmenting by a (non-corresponding) cell value from the right-hand square. The completed exercise will show a geometric square of constant 1728.

The following shows one style of working, although it is otherwise useless because the result is not 1728: (19+4) × (3+5) × (16+1) = 3128.

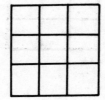

Puzzle 16

Each number in a continuous arithmetical series needed to complete the square increases by 5 – as: 1, 6, 11, etc, although this is not the series. Complete the square if the arithmetical constant is 87.

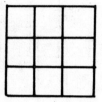

Puzzle 17

The eight missing cell values (from a discontinuous geometric series) are all multiples of 3. When found, they can be placed to show a geometric constant of 5832.

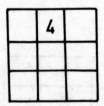

Puzzle 18

Numbers in an irregular arithmetical series can be placed to form a conventional (almost!) magic square. The value 30 is correctly placed, and the magic constant is 111.

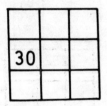

Puzzle 19

The blank multiplication matrix shows the factors for a geometric square, to be completed (not just the matrix!).

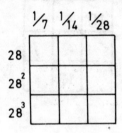

Puzzle 20

Complete this ordinary arithmetical square.

31		
	38	47
	15	

61

Puzzle 21

Complete this ordinary geometric square.

		84
	42	
	252	14

Puzzle 22

This arithmetical square for completion is not based upon a single continuous series. The constant is 36.

10		
		7
	13	

Puzzle 23

This geometrical square for completion (constant 1728) is not based upon a single continuous series.

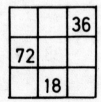

		36
72		
	18	

Puzzle 24

This is only loosely related to magic square matters. If the ten numbers below are correctly placed (one to each of the ten circled vertices) the product (multiply) along each line of the star (four numbers) will be 176,400:

3, 4, 5, 6, 7, 40, 42, 100, 147, and 210.

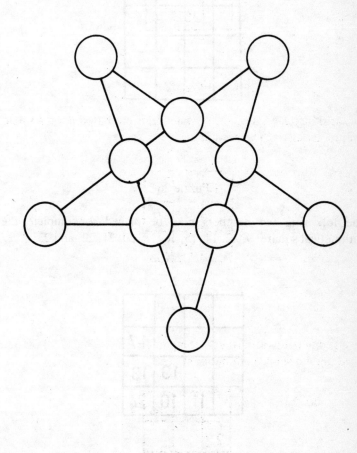

Puzzle 25

Place the 16 numbers 7 to 22 (both inclusive) to form a conventional arithmetical magic square.

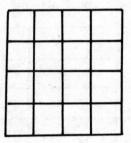

Puzzle 26

The following ten numbers may be placed to complete the arithmetical square: 9, 12, 14, 15, 16, 18, 20, 21, 22, and 23.

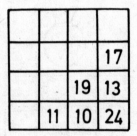

Puzzle 27

The diagram shows the correctly placed highest and lowest cell values in a regular, continuous, series. Form the arithmetical square.

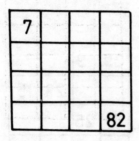

Puzzle 28

The originating series for this orthodox arithmetical square is continuous. Each cell value progresses by an increment of 3 (but the lowest value is not 1). Complete the square.

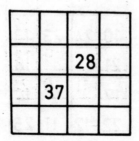

This arithmetical square is based upon an irregular selection of numbers so that, for example, cell values will not balance about the centre point. The square can be completed by finding and placing all of the missing (even) values. The constant is 82 and 29 is the highest value.

29	9		
		23	15
21	25		
		27	19

Puzzle 30

This square is based upon a regular, continuous, arithmetical series (the letter notation will be referred to in the solution).

10	24	23	13
21	a	b	18
17	c		14
22	12	11	25

The cell values in the left hand square are properly placed, but each needs augmenting by a (non-corresponding) cell value from the right hand square. The completed exercise will show a geometric square of constant 2,985,984.

The following shows one way of working, although it is otherwise useless because the result does not equal the constant: $(7+4) \times (9+37) \times (51+2) \times (62+13) = 2,011,350$.

The basic series is not irregular, so that the usual rules will apply.

7	9	51	62
137	20	2	12
6	11	35	1
8	17	3	17

11	4	99	19
199	37	3	2
15	6	25	90
46	13	7	1

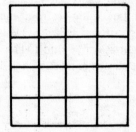

Puzzle 32

When completed, this arithmetical square will show sixteen different prime numbers. Of these, the highest and lowest are shown, correctly placed. The constant is 456.

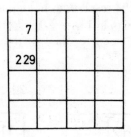

Puzzle 33

In this geometric square, each cell value is found by taking and multiplying together one number from each of the two groups below. Thus, the highest cell value is 119 (i.e. 7 × 17) and the lowest is 2 (i.e. 1 × 2): 2, 3, 5, 7 and 1, 11, 13, 17.

Both 2 and 119 are shown correctly placed.

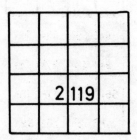

Puzzle 34

This geometric square diagram is based upon an irregular series, so that balancing cell values, and so on, cannot be relied upon. Find and place the four missing values.

68	33	65	171
117			187
57			20
55	36	323	39

Puzzle 35

The dot in each cell value represents either a missing 1 or 2 (units digit). Thus, for example, the top left cell value is either 91 or 92. Next below it is 92 or 91. No cell value is duplicated, and when all of the digits are found and placed, there is a geometric constant of 197,261,064.

9•	5•	32•	13•
9•	46•	22•	2•
56•	16•	1•	18•
4•	5•	23•	39•

The final (units) digit missing from each cell value is either 1 or 6. Therefore, the top right cell value (for example) must be either 851 or 856. Complete the geometric square, which is not based upon a tidy series.

47•	9 •	48•	85•
62 •	66 •	22 •	19 •
48 •	75 •	16 •	30 •
12 •	39 •	103 •	35 •

Puzzle 37

The sixteen cell values are all misplaced prime numbers which, when correctly re-arranged, will show a total of 880 in each line of the arithmetical square.

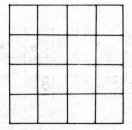

41	173	191	317
359	163	269	23
409	131	257	181
113	419	307	167

The diagram is of an orthodox geometrical square. It needs to be re-arranged into pandiagonal form: cell values along all of the broken diagonals are also to produce the constant.

1	108	54	8
72	6	12	9
24	18	36	3
27	4	2	216

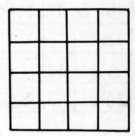

Puzzle 39

This arithmetical square is pandiagonal. Change it to lose only the pandiagonality (i.e. keep the magic quality).

8	50	17	47
41	23	32	26
44	14	53	11
29	35	20	38

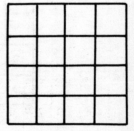

71

These cell values will re-form into an arithmetical, pandiagonal, square.

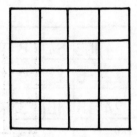

18	6	17	16
12	7	15	21
9	14	10	11
20	24	13	3

Puzzle 41

The eight missing cell values are duplicates of the eight shown. Complete the (arithmetical) square.

	5	13	
	10	11	
3			18
12			6

The four cell values shown, correctly placed, can each be placed three times more (thus filling the square) to show a magic arithmetical constant and, really, an ordinary Latin diagonal square.

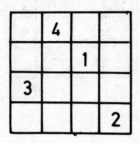

Puzzle 43

The following eight numbers can be placed so that the product of the four cell values along each border is 46,656 (i.e. the geometric constant, really): 2, 3, 4, 9, 24, 54, 72, and 108.

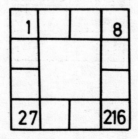

Puzzle 44

Complete this irregular arithmetical square.

51	18	22	
16		50	19
32	15		58
	52	33	14

Puzzle 45

Place the following numbers (powers of 2) to show a matching product in each row (4 cells) and its square root in each column (2 cells): 1, 2, 4, 8, 16, 32, 64, and 128.

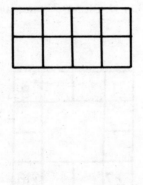

Puzzle 46

In this arithmetical square for completion, each cell value equals the total formed by taking one number from each of the following two groups of prime numbers: 3, 5, 7, 11, and 13, 23, 37, 47.

The lowest cell value (16 = 3 + 13) and the highest (58 = 11 + 47) are each shown correctly placed.

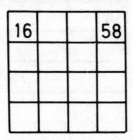

Puzzle 47

In this geometric square for completion, each cell value equals the product formed by multiplying one number from each of the following two groups of prime numbers: 3, 5, 7, 11, and 13, 23, 37, 47.

The lowest cell value (39 = 3 × 13) and the highest (517 = 11 × 47) are each shown correctly placed.

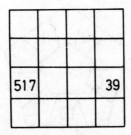

Puzzle 48

Compile an arithmetical magic square, using the numbers 1 to 16, ensuring that these two numbers appear as shown.

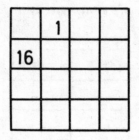

Puzzle 49

When the empty corner cells are filled with the right numbers, the total will be 88 along each side of the pentagon (three cells). Thus, if we try 30 at the top (empty) corner cell, the following series results:

30,11,47 – 47,12,29 – 29,13,46 – 46,20,22 – 22,10,56.

As 30 (first) is different from 56 (last) we need to start with a different number so that they may be equal.

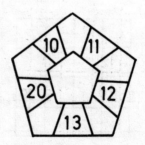

Place 13 even numbers to complete this regular arithmetical square and show its constant of 70.

15	11		23	19
21				25
3				7
9	5		17	13

Puzzle 51

Complete this conventional, associative, arithmetical square and show its constant of 95.

	11	13	20	
	12		26	
	18	25	27	

Puzzle 52

The completed square will show an arithmetical constant of 13 by entering either 2 or 3 in each cell. Each line has the same constituent numbers. A Latin square problem, really.

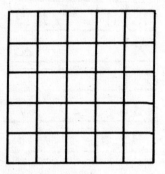

Puzzle 53

The completed square will show an arithmetical constant of 13 by entering either 1, 2, or 7 in each cell. Each line has the same constituent numbers.

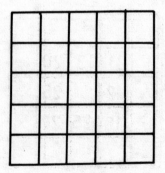

Puzzle 54

Arrange the natural number series 1 to 25 into a pandiagonal arithmetical square, with 1 and 25 at the positions shown.

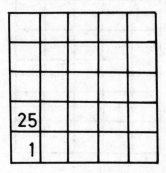

Puzzle 55

Produce a conventional, continuous series, arithmetical square with cell increment of 3 and cell values that balance at 88.

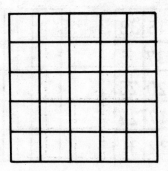

Puzzle 56

Produce a conventional, continuous series, arithmetical square having 7 as the lowest cell value and a constant of 395.

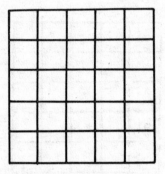

Puzzle 57

An arithmetical, random number, square. Each of the two (four sided) borders show all of its cell values, but no value is in its right position within its border. The centre cell (46) is correct.

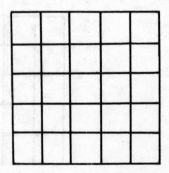

Puzzle 58

Re-arrange the given random numbers into an arithmetical and pandiagonal square.

5	8	10	23	46
39	40	36	12	37
20	47	34	30	31
16	9	22	35	24
26	7	33	32	13

Puzzle 59

Complete this entirely ordinary geometric square of constant 60,466,176.

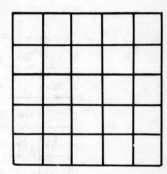

This square is based upon random numbers. The missing final (units) digit in each cell value is either 1 or 2 (e.g. the top left hand cell value is either 731 or 732). The geometric constant is so splendid that it's worth a line of its own: 229,020,095,304.

73•	18•	23•	8•	9•
89•	1•	39•	60•	9•
32•	30•	35•	13•	5•
5•	56•	4•	16•	116•
2•	62•	17•	22•	46•

Puzzle 61

All of the odd numbers are missing in this ordinary arithmetical square (i.e. it is formed from a continuous series).

	76		28	
			46	52
16	22		64	70
34	40			
	58		10	

Puzzle 62

Place 13 odd numbers to complete this regular arithmetical square of constant 95.

20	16		28	24
26				30
8				12
14	10		22	18

Puzzle 63

Complete this regular geometric square whose magic constant is: 61,917,364,224.

				192
			64	36
		5184	12	216

Puzzle 64

As with the cell values shown, the missing twelve values are also different prime numbers (counting 1 as prime). When found and correctly placed, the arithmetical constant will be seen as 647 (also prime).

	163	137	83	
53				107
229		23		257
7				17
	89	1	197	

Puzzle 65

A change from magic squares! The knights' move in the game of chess is 'two squares along and one to the side' (in any direction). A knight on cell 1 of our diagram may then go to cell 2, then to cell 3, cell 4, and so on. Given this start, the aim is to visit each cell once in a tour ending at cell 25.

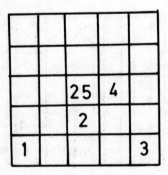

In this geometric, pandiagonal, square, each cell value will be found by taking the product of two numbers, one from each of the two groups below. Thus, the highest cell value (shown in its right place) is 117 (i.e. 9 × 13) and the lowest is 2 (i.e. 1 × 2): 1,4,6,8,9 and 2,5,7,9,13.

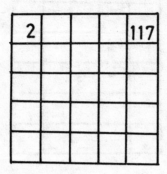

Puzzle 67

The diagram shows the proper position of the lowest cell value in a continuous arithmetical series. When this is found and correctly entered, the magic constant will show itself as 255.

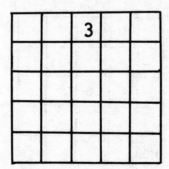

Puzzle 68

The five cell values shown are correctly placed. Each can be placed four more times to show an arithmetical constant in the usual manner. A Latin square problem.

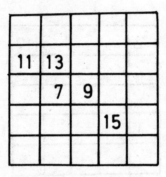

Puzzle 69

This arithmetical (pandiagonal) square will show 25 different prime numbers when completed. Of these, the highest and lowest are shown in their right places. The constant is 2201.

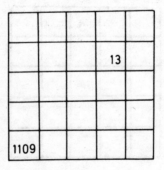

Puzzle 70

When totally re-arranged (no fraction is in its right cell) the magic geometric constant will be seen as 9/70400 (or, as a decimal fraction, about 0.000127840909). The cell values are not based upon any regular series.

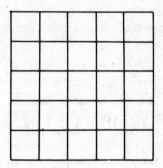

$\frac{12}{55}$	$\frac{1}{16}$	$\frac{3}{22}$	$\frac{1}{22}$	$\frac{2}{5}$
$\frac{7}{20}$	$\frac{8}{25}$	$\frac{3}{8}$	$\frac{9}{44}$	$\frac{1}{48}$
$\frac{1}{10}$	$\frac{1}{12}$	$\frac{9}{28}$	$\frac{3}{14}$	$\frac{3}{32}$
$\frac{21}{56}$	$\frac{12}{35}$	$\frac{3}{10}$	$\frac{21}{88}$	$\frac{1}{5}$
$\frac{7}{64}$	$\frac{1}{15}$	$\frac{1}{4}$	$\frac{1}{14}$	$\frac{7}{16}$

Place the numbers 1 to 15 so that each row (5 cells) totals to 40, and each column (3 cells) to 24 (i.e. 40 × 3/5).

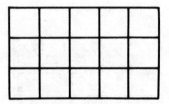

Puzzle 72

The nine missing numbers (all between 1 and 25) will form a third order square to complete an equally ordinary fifth order arithmetical square.

19	18	4	1	23
21				5
2				24
20				6
3	8	22	25	7

Puzzle 73

In this arithmetical square, one cell in each row shows twice its true value (five incorrect cells in all). Thus, the top right hand corner cell might have a true value of 5, rather than 10. Next below it might be a cell value of 6, rather than 12; and so on. Complete the square.

52	42	18	34	10
38	4	60	46	12
50	16	64	8	24
2	28	44	20	72
14	80	6	22	48

Puzzle 74

Compile an arithmetical magic square (1 to 25), ensuring that these two values appear where shown.

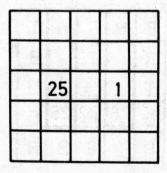

Form the natural number series 5 to 29 into an arithmetical magic square which, as well, shows a 3 × 3 arithmetical magic square in the nine central cells.

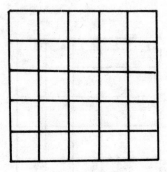

Puzzle 76

This is the first of a few Latin square puzzles with letters instead of numbers.

By correctly entering, in the outlined initial letter, the seven letters of HERBERT, a diagonal Latin square can be shown.

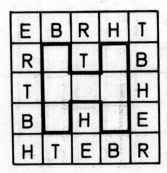

Puzzle 77

Complete this geometric square.

1	6		216	1296
108	648		3	18
162	4		144	27
72	432		2	12

Puzzle 78

By correctly entering, in the outlined initial, the seven letters of UKULELE, a diagonal Latin square can be shown.

U	Q	E	L	K
Q		K		U
K		Q		L
E				Q
L	K	U	Q	E

Puzzle 79

Complete this irregular arithmetical square:

	29	28	39	18
36	25	38	12	
10	26		22	45
37	42	17		34
31		20	57	14

Puzzle 80

Produce a conventional, continuous series, arithmetical square having 3 as the lowest cell value and a constant of 438.

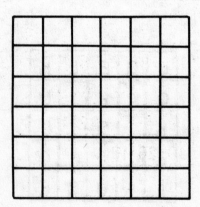

The six cell values shown, correctly placed, can each be placed five times more (appearing once in each line, and filling the square) to show an arithmetical constant of 21.

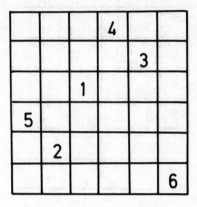

Puzzle 82

All of the odd numbers are missing from this basic (1 to 36) arithmetical square.

	32	4			6
12	8		28		
			16	20	24
18			22	14	
30	26	10			
		34		2	36

Puzzle 83

The completed square will show an arithmetical constant of 14 by entering either 1, 2, or 3 in each cell. Each line has the same constituent numbers (a Latin square problem).

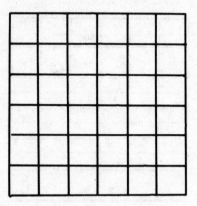

Puzzle 84

A combination of the numbers 2 and 7 (one or other entered into each cell) will show a geometric constant of 784 (a Latin square, really). Each line has the same constituent numbers.

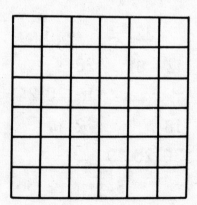

Puzzle 85

In the diagram, dots replace the units digits that are even (i.e. 0, 2, 4, 6, or 8). Thus, the top left cell value might be: 40, 42, 44, 46, or 48.

The square is arithmetical and based upon a regular series although, plainly, the construction method given in Part I has been varied.

4•	61	55	5•	7•	49
31	25	91	7•	3•	8•
10•	10•	•	19	7	103
13	1•	9•	109	97	1•
85	79	2•	37	8•	2•
6•	5•	73	4•	43	67

By placing the following cell values, complete this border from an arithmetical square: 7, 10, 13, 16, 22, 37, 40, 55, 58, 73, 76, 91, 97, 100, 103, and 106.

109					94
19					4

Each of the nine sub-squares (four cells each) is correct in itself but, to show a normal geometric square, the sub-squares must be totally re-arranged (i.e. no sub-square is correctly placed in the puzzle diagram.)

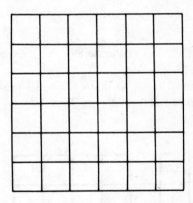

80	480	25	48	100	24
30	160	32	2	600	300
2400	150	16	75	4	8
96	400	50	3	12	200
6	800	120	60	5	10
1200	1	40	20	15	240

Puzzle 88

Form the natural number series 1 to 36 into an arithmetical magic square which, as well, shows a fourth order arithmetical square in the central 4 × 4 cells.

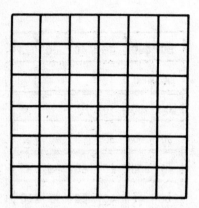

Puzzle 89

Place the numbers 1 to 24 so that each row (6 cells) totals to 75, and each column (4 cells) to 50 (i.e. 75 × 4/6).

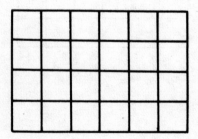

By correctly entering, in the outlined initial letter, the eight letters of FAMILIAR, an ordinary (not diagonal) Latin square can be shown (i.e. ignore repeated cell values along either diagonal).

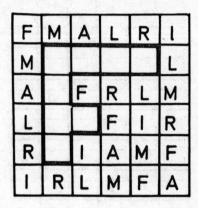

Another knight's tour. Starting from cell 1 of our diagram, a knight goes to cell 2, then to cells 3, 4, and 5. Given this start, the aim is to visit each cell once in a tour ending at cell 36. Unlike the fifth order tour, this one is called 're-entrant' because another step after the last takes us back to the starting point (cell 1).

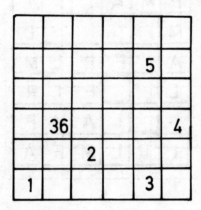

Puzzle 92

Compile an arithmetical magic square (1 to 49), ensuring that these first and last numbers appear as shown.

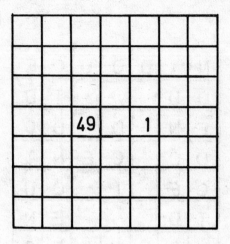

As an incantation, COCONUT NUDE is less well known than
'open sesame' but its eleven letters will, if correctly placed in the
outlined initial, reveal magical qualities – i.e. that the square is a
Latin diagonal.

N	T	D	O	U	C	E
O	U				T	D
E	N	D		U	C	
D	O		C	E	N	T
C	E		T		O	U
T	D				E	N
U	C	E	N	T	D	O

When the outlined fylfot is correctly filled, the square (1 to 49) will show itself as being arithmetical, pandiagonal but, clearly, not associative.

48	9	26	36	4	21	31
7				12		39
8	25	42		20		47
16						6
24		2		29	46	14
32		10				15
40	1	18	35	45	13	23

The 25 central cells for this seventh order arithmetical square (1 to 49) show a fifth order square. Place the 24 missing values around the edge, thus completing the square.

	29	36	13	20	27	
	35	17	19	26	28	
	16	18	25	32	34	
	22	24	31	33	15	
	23	30	37	14	21	

By correctly entering, in the outlined initial letter, the ten letters of JOURDANTON (a town in Texas, USA), a diagonal Latin square can be shown if, also, the square's border is completed.

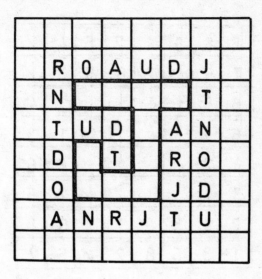

To show an eighth order diagonal Latin square, correctly fill the sixteen empty cells by twice using each number in the natural series 1 to 8 (both inclusive, of course).

8	6	3	1	7	5	4	2
7	5	4	2	8	6	3	1
6	8					2	4
5	7					1	3
4	2					8	6
3	1					7	5
2	4	5	7	1	3	6	8
1	3	6	8	2	4	5	7

Puzzle 98

Complete this ordinary diagonal Latin square.

i	h	g	f	e	d	c	b	a
c	b	a	i	h	g	f	e	d
f	e						h	g
h	g		e	d	f		a	c
b	a						d	f
e	d	f	b	a	c		g	i
g	i						c	b
a	c	b	g	i	h	d	f	e
d	f	e	a	c	b	g	i	h

By correctly entering, in the outlined initial letter, the seven letters of LIMPOPO (an African river), a diagonal Latin square can be shown if, also, the border is completed.

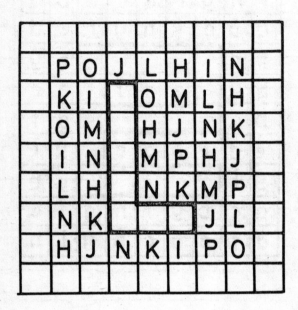

Puzzle 100

Complete this semi-diagonal Latin square (i.e. there are repeated cell values along *one* main diagonal.)

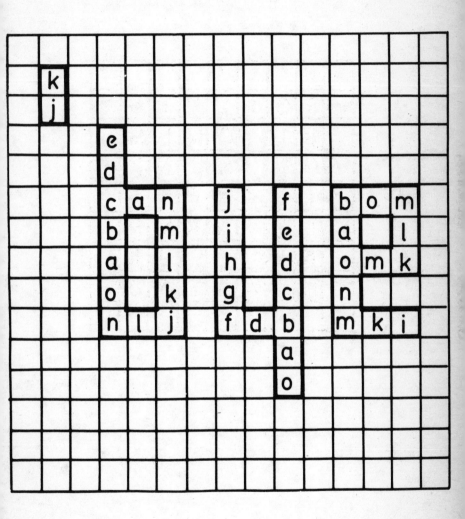

PART II
(Solutions)

Solution 1

10	3	8
5	7	9
6	11	4

Solution 2

17	10	15
12	14	16
13	18	11

Solution 3

24	3	18
9	15	21
12	27	6

Solution 4

25	4	19
10	16	22
13	28	7

Solution 5

Note: the magic constant must be 99, i.e.:
$$(48+18) \times 3/2 = 99$$

48	13	38
23	33	43
28	53	18

Solution 6

Note: the product of any balanced pair will be:
$$13824^{2/3} = 576$$
(e.g. 3×192, 12×48, etc.)

192	$1\frac{1}{2}$	48
6	24	96
12	384	3

Solution 7

43	22	34
24	33	42
32	44	23

Solution 8

18	11	16
13	15	17
14	19	12

Solution 9

Note: the product of any balanced pair will be: $216^{2/3} = 36$

12	1	18
9	6	4
2	36	3

Solution 10

109	31	79
43	73	103
67	115	37

Solution 11

87	17	67
37	57	77
47	97	27

Solution 12

53	13	48
33	38	43
28	63	23

Solution 13

Note: from principles, the total of the lowest and highest cell values will be: 141 × 2/3 = 94. Hence, the highest is 75 (i.e. 94 − 19) and the increment per cell is found from: (75 − 19)/8 = 7.

The generating series must then be 19, 26, 33 . . . 75.

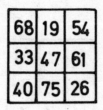

Solution 14

Note: the total of the cell values in both squares is 261, so that we find the constant: 261/3 = 87. And, from principles, the total of the highest and lowest cell values must be 58 (i.e. 87 × 2/3 = 58). Because, in an odd order square, the highest and lowest values are always in the same line, the central cell value must be 29 (i.e. 87 − 58). Solution should then proceed reasonably well.

38	17	32
23	29	35
26	41	20

Note: from usual principles:
   (a) (lowest value) × (highest value) = $1728^{2/3}$ = 144
   (b) centre cell value = 1728/144   = 12
The lowest value must be less than 12 and, after rejecting 1, 2, and 3 as possibilities, 4 is seen as the lowest cell value. Which gives 36 (i.e. 144/4) as the highest value, and so on.

24	4	18
9	12	16
8	36	6

Solution 16

Note: (lowest value) + (highest value) = 87 × 2/3 = 58.
   The centre cell value then becomes 29 (i.e. 87 − 58) and solution can proceed.

44	9	34
19	29	39
24	49	14

Solution 17

Note: for a start the highest cell value $= \dfrac{5832^{2/3}}{4} = 81$.

54	4	27
9	18	36
12	81	6

Solution 18

Note: just a gentle reminder that a square can be turned on its side!

41	36	34
30	37	44
40	38	33

Solution 19

Note: by knowing the factors, we can easily shortcut to the constant: $28^5 \times 1/7 \times 1/14 = 175,616$.

1568	4	28
1	56	3136
112	784	2

Note: by applying the letter notation to the matching (blank) cells of the puzzle diagram:

$$31 + 38 + b = 15 + a + b$$

whence: $54 = a$

Then:

$$54 + 38 + c = 47 + b + c$$

whence: $45 = b$

The constant is, then, 114 and the solution follows.

31	61	22^c
29	38	47
54^a	15	45^b

Solution 21

Note: by applying the given letter notation to the corresponding blank cells of the puzzle diagram:

$$84ab = (42 \times 14)a$$
$$b = \frac{42 \times 14}{84} = 7.$$

The constant is then found, easily, as 74,088 and solution can proceed.

126^a	7^b	84
28	42	63
21	252	14

Note: we apply the letter notation to matching cell positions in the puzzle diagram:

$$b + d = 26 \ (\text{i.e. } 36 - 10)$$
$$a + d = 23 \ (\text{i.e. } 36 - 13)$$
$$c + d = \underline{29} \ (\text{i.e. } 36 - 7)$$

Total: $a + b + c + 3d = \overline{78}$

Subtract: $a + b + c\ \ \ = 36$ (the constant)

Difference: $\ \ \ \ \ \ \ \ \ 3d = \overline{42}$ (i.e. 'd' is 14)

Solution should follow easily.

10	11	15 ^{c}
17	12 ^{b}	7
^{a} 9	13	14 ^{d}

Solution 23

Note: we apply the letter notation to matching cell positions in the puzzle diagram:

$ad = 24$ (i.e. 1728/72), $bd = 48$ (i.e. 1728/36) and $cd = 96$ (i.e. 1728/18).

Then: $d^3 = \dfrac{24 \times 48 \times 96}{1728} = 64$ (i.e. 'd' is 4).

The solution should follow easily.

^{a} 6	8	36
72	12 ^{b}	2
^{d} 4	18	24 ^{c}

Note: the product of the ten values can be found, also, by applying the power of 5/2 to the constant:

product = $176,400^{5/2}$ = $1.30691232 \times 10^{13}$ (exactly).

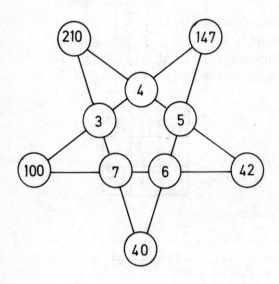

Solution 25

7	21	20	10
18	12	13	15
14	16	17	11
19	9	8	22

9	23	22	12
20	14	15	17
16	18	19	13
21	11	10	24

Solution 27

Note: the generating series must proceed by increments of 5 because, using the given values (highest and lowest) and noting the fact of 15 increments:

$$(82 - 7)/ 15 = 5$$

The series then becomes: 7, 12, 17 . . . 82.

7	77	72	22
62	32	37	47
42	52	57	27
67	17	12	82

Note: we use balanced pair value of 65, and the fact that there are 15 increments of 3 (i.e. 45) to indulge in simple algebra:

$$\text{highest value} - \text{lowest} = 45$$
$$\text{highest value} + \text{lowest} = \underline{65}$$

By addition: (highest) × 2　　　　= 110 (i.e. highest is 55)

Which makes the lowest value 10, and the generating series:

$$10, 13, 16, 19 \ldots 52, 55.$$

But there are other ways to the same result.

10	52	49	19
43	25	28	34
31	37	40	22
46	16	13	55

Solution 29

Note: the extreme left-hand column (for example and ease of working) in the puzzle diagram shows one of two least deficits (32) i.e.:

$$82 - (21+29) = 32$$

We may then easily note down the only possible pairs to suit:

(and)	18	20	22	24	26	28
	14	12	10	8	6	4

And so on, but there may well be a better way with this one.

29	9	18	26
24	20	23	15
21	25	14	22
8	28	27	19

Note: the constant is clearly 70 and, using the letter notation with brief, but simple, algebra:

$$a + b = 70 - (21+18) = 31$$
$$b + c = 70 - (22+13) = 35$$
$$a + c = 70 - (24+12) = 34$$

whence $2b = (31+35) - 34 = 32$ (i.e. 'b' is 16)

The solution should proceed without difficulty.

10	24	23	13
21	ᵃ15	ᵇ16	18
17	ᶜ19	20	14
22	12	11	25

Solution 31

Note: from the associativity principle, balanced pairs will have a value (product) of 1728 (i.e. $2,985,984^{1/2}$). If we consider one of the central pairs (20 and 35) we may work through the available cell values from the right hand square to see which, when added to 35 and with this total divided into 1728, gives an integer (whole number) result.

For example: $1728/(35+13) = 36$ (shown below).

This drill gives the following possible cell values: 36, 48, 54, or 72.

Then, by trial:

$$1728/36 = 48 \qquad \text{(and } 48 - 20 = 28\text{)}$$
$$1728/48 = 36 \qquad \text{(and } 36 - 20 = 16\text{)}$$
$$1728/54 = 32 \qquad \text{(and } 32 - 20 = 12\text{)}$$
$$1728/72 = 24 \qquad \text{(and } 24 - 20 = 4\text{)} *$$

(*) because 4 is the only available cell value in the right hand square, the central pair under consideration must be (24 × 72).

The solution becomes easier as the values are found.

8	108	54	64
144	24	48	18
96	36	72	12
27	32	16	216

7	167	89	193
229	53	107	67
137	73	223	23
83	163	37	173

Solution 33

Note: the product of the eight generating numbers is 510,510 (the geometric constant). The partially complete row can be finalised by finding two values whose product equals 2145:

$$510,510/(2 \times 119) = 2145.$$

Plainly, 39 and 55 fit the bill; which should give a fair start to completion.

5	91	22	51
34	33	65	7
39	2	119	55
77	85	3	26

Solution 34

Note: this approach can be used to find any one of the four missing cell values. The other three can then be entered, almost at sight.

The geometric constant is 24,942,060 and, for cell 'b', from simple algebra considerations:

$$b^2 = \frac{33 \times 36 \times 24,942,060}{117 \times 187 \times 171 \times 55} = 144 \text{ (i.e. 'b' is 12)}$$

68	33	65	171
117	95	b 12	187
57	221	99	20
55	36	323	39

Solution 35

Note: divide the constant by possible cell values to see which are factors. For example, the constant divided by 322 shows an integer (whole number) result, while division by 321 doesn't. So that 322 is the required cell value. Continue with others in the same line. Occasionally, both possible values may be factors of the constant; e.g. both 51 and 52 are factors of 197,261,064. Not a real problem, though.

91	51	322	132
92	462	221	21
561	161	12	182
42	52	231	391

Solution 36

Note: first find the geometric constant. In any line of four cells there will be 16 possibilities e.g. (left hand column):
(471 or 476) × (621 or 626) × (481 or 486) × (121 or 126)

A repeat of this procedure with any other line should throw up a matching constant: 17,914,891,176.

Next, divide the constant by possible cell values to see if they are factors; as they must be for a solution – much as in an earlier puzzle, in fact.

476	91	486	851
621	666	221	196
481	756	161	306
126	391	1036	351

Solution 37

23	257	409	191
181	419	167	113
317	163	131	269
359	41	173	307

Solution 38

Note: the rule for converting to pandiagonal form is given in Part I.

1	108	8	54
72	6	9	12
27	4	216	2
24	18	3	36

Solution 39

Note; the rule for converting to pandiagonal form can be applied.

8	50	47	17
41	23	26	32
29	35	38	20
44	14	11	53

Solution 40

Note: here are two possibilities from many.

3	21	12	18
20	10	11	13
15	9	24	6
16	14	7	17

12	18	3	21
11	13	20	10
24	6	15	9
7	17	16	14

Solution 41

Note: the given cell values must total to half that for the full square. This makes 39 the constant and removes most of the difficulty.

11	5	13	10
13	10	11	5
3	6	12	18
12	18	3	6

Solution 42

1	4	2	3
2	3	1	4
3	2	4	1
4	1	3	2

Solution 43

Note: the product of balanced cells is 216; select pairs to suit.

1	108	54	8
72			9
24			3
27	4	2	216

Solution 44

Note: by finding the constant we can quickly solve. Applying the letter notation to the puzzle diagram:

$$52 + 33 + 14 + a = 15 + 50 + a + b$$
$$99 + a = 65 + a + b$$

whence: $\qquad 34 = b$.

The constant must then be 125 and the solution follows easily.

51	18	22	34^{b}
16	40	50	19
32	15	20	58
26^{a}	52	33	14

Solution 45

1	64	32	8
128	2	4	16

Solution 46

16	28	44	58
54	48	26	18
34	20	52	40
42	50	24	30

Solution 47

111	235	91	253
161	143	141	185
517	259	115	39
65	69	407	329

Solution 48

Note: there is no special system here.

7	1	14	12
16	10	5	3
9	15	4	6
2	8	11	13

Solution 49

Note: the right series results if a new starting number is the simple average of any trial starting number and its resulting last number: $(30+56)/2 = 43$.

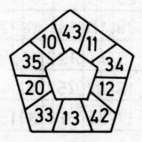

Solution 50

15	11	2	23	19
21	12	8	4	25
22	18	14	10	6
3	24	20	16	7
9	5	26	17	13

Solution 51

Note: from principles (equal increments along the SW/NE diagonal) the central value can only be 19. The only series to suit the conditions is easily found as: 7, 8, 9, . . . 30, 31.

23	30	7	14	21
29	11	13	20	22
10	12	19	26	28
16	18	25	27	9
17	24	31	8	15

Solution 52

Note: it is not hard to find, first, that each line must show (three times) the digit 3 and (twice) the digit 2. No other arrangement will suit.

2	2	3	3	3
3	3	3	2	2
3	2	2	3	3
2	3	3	3	2
3	3	2	2	3

Solution 53

7	2	2	1	1
1	1	7	2	2
2	2	1	1	7
1	7	2	2	1
2	1	1	7	2

Solution 54

7	20	3	11	24
13	21	9	17	5
19	2	15	23	6
25	8	16	4	12
1	14	22	10	18

Solution 55

Note: we need to find an arithmetical series that fits the conditions. The common formula for a continuous arithmetical series will apply, but it shortens to (where 'N' is the number of terms in the series):

$$\text{lowest cell value} = \frac{\text{Balance value} - (N - 1)\text{ increment value}}{2}$$

$$\text{(in this case)} = \frac{88 - (24 \times 3)}{2} = 8$$

The required series is then: 8, 11, 14, . . . 80.

56	77	8	29	50
74	20	26	47	53
17	23	44	65	71
35	41	62	68	14
38	59	80	11	32

Solution 56

Note: cell values must balance at : $395 \times 2/5 = 158$

Then, by transposing a simple formula already given:

$$\text{increment value} = \frac{\text{Balance value} - (\text{lowest cell value})2}{N - 1}$$

(in this case) $= \dfrac{158 - (7 \times 2)}{24} = 6$

The generating series is: 7, 13, 19, ... 151.

103	145	7	49	91
139	31	43	85	97
25	37	79	121	133
61	73	115	127	19
67	109	151	13	55

Solution 57

35	24	23	34	13
31	20	33	7	38
5	21	46	17	40
32	37	12	19	29
26	27	15	52	9

Solution 58

I don't think this is easy!

34	20	35	8	30
31	16	24	47	9
37	36	5	39	10
13	33	23	26	32
12	22	40	7	46

Solution 59

Note: Because of the balanced cell idea, the centre cell must be 36, i.e.:

$$(12 \times 108)^{1/2} = 36$$

There must therefore be a progression factor of 3 along the SW/NE diagonal:

$$4, 12, 36, 108, \text{ and } 324$$

The solution should proceed reasonably well.

24	432	1	18	324
144	81	6	108	8
27	2	36	648	48
162	12	216	16	9
4	72	1296	3	54

Solution 60

Note: divide the constant by either of the two possible values for any cell. The right result must be an integer (whole number). Repeat the procedure to complete the line, and as necessary to complete the square. For example:

constant/891 = an integer (i.e. 257,037,144)

constant/892 = (not an integer, so that 892 is not a cell value)

Sometimes, with this sort of problem, each of the possible cell values is an integer; this hardly seems to be a real snag.

731	182	231	81	92
891	12	391	602	91
322	301	351	132	51
52	561	42	161	1161
21	621	172	221	462

Solution 61

55	76	7	28	49
73	19	25	46	52
16	22	43	64	70
34	40	61	67	13
37	58	79	10	31

Solution 62

20	16	7	28	24
26	17	13	9	30
27	23	19	15	11
8	29	25	21	12
14	10	31	22	18

Solution 63

Note: the value of any balanced pair will be:
$$61,917,364,224^{2/5} = 20,736.$$

This is a nasty piece of figurework, but the result allows, because of balanced cell values, six unknown cell values to be entered at once.

96	1728	4	72	1296
576	324	24	432	32
108	8	144	2592	192
648	48	864	64	36
16	288	5184	12	216

Solution 64

191	163	137	83	73
53	67	263	157	107
229	101	23	37	257
7	227	223	173	17
167	89	1	197	193

Solution 65

7	12	17	22	5
18	23	6	11	16
13	8	25	4	21
24	19	2	15	10
1	14	9	20	3

Note: the product of the generating numbers is 14,152,320; the magic constant.

The top row can be completed by finding three cell values whose product equals 60,480 i.e.:

$$\frac{14,152,320}{2 \times 117} = 60,480$$

2	20	42	72	117
54	104	18	5	28
45	7	36	78	16
52	12	40	63	9
56	81	13	8	30

Solution 67

Cell balance value = 255 × 2/5 = 102

Thus, the highest cell value must be 99 (i.e. 102 − 3) and the increment in the generating series:

$$\frac{99 - 3}{24} = 4$$

And this must be the series: 3, 7, 11, . . . 99.

67	95	3	31	59
91	19	27	55	63
15	23	51	79	87
39	47	75	83	11
43	71	99	7	35

Solution 68

7	9	11	13	15
11	13	15	7	9
15	7	9	11	13
9	11	13	15	7
13	15	7	9	11

Solution 69

I don't see an easy way, even though we have two values along the same diagonal. Perhaps the sheer number of possible arrangements pushes the result toward the insoluble.

19	263	227	1061	631
179	1031	619	13	359
613	109	311	149	1019
281	137	1013	709	61
1109	661	31	269	131

Solution 70

$\frac{3}{14}$	$\frac{3}{10}$	$\frac{7}{16}$	$\frac{1}{10}$	$\frac{1}{22}$
$\frac{7}{64}$	$\frac{12}{55}$	$\frac{1}{14}$	$\frac{1}{5}$	$\frac{3}{8}$
$\frac{1}{15}$	$\frac{1}{4}$	$\frac{3}{32}$	$\frac{21}{88}$	$\frac{12}{35}$
$\frac{9}{44}$	$\frac{21}{56}$	$\frac{8}{25}$	$\frac{1}{12}$	$\frac{1}{16}$
$\frac{2}{5}$	$\frac{1}{48}$	$\frac{3}{22}$	$\frac{9}{28}$	$\frac{7}{20}$

Solution 71

2	6	12	11	9
15	13	8	3	1
7	5	4	10	14

Solution 72

19	18	4	1	23
21	16	9	14	5
2	11	13	15	24
20	12	17	10	6
3	8	22	25	7

Note: the top (say) row total is 156. This must be too great by either 26, 21, 9, 17, or 5 (i.e. half the individual cell values). We may then set out possible row totals with, for comparison, the results from cognate arithmetic carried out upon the second (or any other) row:

1st row, possible totals: 130   135   147   139   151
2nd row, possible totals: 141   158   130   137   154.

The magic constant must be 130, and our difficulties vanish.

26	42	18	34	10
38	4	30	46	12
50	16	32	8	24
2	28	44	20	36
14	40	6	22	48

Solution 74

Note: there is a system to the construction method that the solution diagram can reveal.

3	16	9	22	15
20	8	21	14	2
7	25	13	1	19
24	12	5	18	6
11	4	17	10	23

Solution 75

23	6	24	5	27
8	20	13	18	26
22	15	17	19	12
25	16	21	14	9
7	28	10	29	11

Solution 76

E	B	R	H	T
R	H	T	E	B
T	E	B	R	H
B	R	H	T	E
H	T	E	B	R

Solution 77

Note: some preliminary algebra (very simple!) gives the constant.

1	6	36	216	1296
108	648	16	3	18
48	9	54	324	8
162	4	24	144	27
72	432	81	2	12

Solution 78

U	Q	E	L	K
Q	L	K	E	U
K	E	Q	U	L
E	U	L	K	Q
L	K	U	Q	E

Note: We apply the letter notation to the puzzle diagram to find the constant (K):

$$39 + a + b + c = K \text{ (i.e. along one diagonal)}$$

And, for three columns:

$$114 + a = K, \ 103 + b = K, \text{ and } 130 + c = K$$

Columns total: $347 + a + b + c = 3K$

Diagonal   : $39 + a + b + c = K$ (subtract)

Difference : $308 \qquad\qquad = 2K$

$$154 \qquad\qquad = K$$

Which should dispose of the difficulties.

40ᵃ	29	28	39	18
36	25	38	12	43
10	26	51ᵇ	22	45
37	42	17	24ᶜ	34
31	32	20	57	14

Note; this is interesting (well, it's all interesting, of course); although a sixth order square cannot be made associative with a continuous series, we may calculate the notional cell balance value and use it in a simple solution formula given earlier:

Notional balance value = $438 \times 2/6 = 146$

Increment value $= \dfrac{\text{Balance value} - (\text{lowest cell value})2}{N - 1}$

(in this case) $= \dfrac{146 - (3 \times 2)}{35} = 4$

The generating series is, therefore: 3, 7, 11, . . . 143.

143	127	11	15	19	123
47	115	35	111	103	27
51	55	87	83	67	95
75	91	63	59	79	71
99	43	107	39	31	119
23	7	135	131	139	3

Solution 81

3	6	2	4	5	1
6	5	4	1	3	2
2	4	1	5	6	3
5	3	6	2	1	4
1	2	3	6	4	5
4	1	5	3	2	6

Solution 82

1	32	4	33	35	6
12	8	27	28	11	25
19	17	15	16	20	24
18	23	21	22	14	13
30	26	10	9	29	7
31	5	34	3	2	36

Solution 83

1	2	2	3	3	3
3	3	3	2	2	1
2	3	3	1	2	3
2	1	3	2	3	3
3	2	1	3	3	2
3	3	2	3	1	2

Solution 84

Note: a breakdown of 784 into its prime factors shows how many of each digit are needed:

$$2 \times 2 \times 2 \times 2 \times 7 \times 7 = 784.$$

2	2	2	2	7	7
7	2	7	2	2	2
2	2	7	2	7	2
2	2	2	7	2	7
7	7	2	2	2	2
2	7	2	7	2	2

Solution 85

Note: even with a sixth order square it is worthwhile checking for cell value balance along the main diagonals; which should give a start.

46	61	55	58	70	49
31	25	91	76	34	82
100	106	4	19	7	103
13	16	94	109	97	10
85	79	22	37	88	28
64	52	73	40	43	67

Note; remember that any sixth order square is necessarily non-associative.

The total of the sixteen given values is 904. When added to the four corner values (counted twice) the total is 1356. The constant (total along each edge) is then 339 (i.e. 1356/4). Select from the values given.

109	97	10	13	16	94
37					22
40					73
58					55
76					91
19	7	103	100	106	4

Solution 87

2400	150	4	8	16	75
96	400	12	200	50	3
5	10	120	60	80	480
15	240	40	20	30	160
25	48	100	24	6	800
32	2	600	300	1200	1

Solution 88

36	2	3	7	32	31
29	26	12	13	23	8
27	15	21	20	18	10
9	19	17	16	22	28
4	14	24	25	11	33
6	35	34	30	5	1

Solution 89

1	2	3	22	23	24
19	20	21	4	5	6
18	17	16	9	8	7
12	11	10	15	14	13

Solution 90

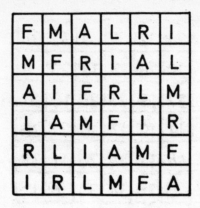

F	M	A	L	R	I
M	F	R	I	A	L
A	I	F	R	L	M
L	A	M	F	I	R
R	L	I	A	M	F
I	R	L	M	F	A

Solution 91

Note: by starting as specified, there is only one possible path to cell number 36, I believe. To compensate, there is a characteristic and pleasing pattern formed if we join, with straight lines, the consecutive numbers in the solution diagram (as shown).

10	21	6	31	8	19
35	32	9	20	5	30
22	11	34	7	18	15
33	36	25	16	29	4
12	23	2	27	14	17
1	26	13	24	3	28

Solution 92

4	29	12	37	20	45	28
35	11	36	19	44	27	3
10	42	18	43	26	2	34
41	17	49	25	1	33	9
16	48	24	7	32	8	40
47	23	6	31	14	39	15
22	5	30	13	38	21	46

Solution 93

N	T	D	O	U	C	E
O	U	C	E	N	T	D
E	N	T	D	O	U	C
D	O	U	C	E	N	T
C	E	N	T	D	O	U
T	D	O	U	C	E	N
U	C	E	N	T	D	O

Solution 94

Note: by rearranging two sections of rows, and two sections of columns, the completed square (being pandiagonal) can be made associative (cell value 1 will appear at top row centre; cell value 49 will appear at bottom row centre). This knowledge hardly helps towards a solution.

48	9	26	36	4	21	31
7	17	34	44	12	22	39
8	25	42	3	20	30	47
16	33	43	11	28	38	6
24	41	2	19	29	46	14
32	49	10	27	37	5	15
40	1	18	35	45	13	23

Solution 95

46	1	5	39	6	38	40
7	29	36	13	20	27	43
48	35	17	19	26	28	2
8	16	18	25	32	34	42
47	22	24	31	33	15	3
9	23	30	37	14	21	41
10	49	45	11	44	12	4

Solution 96

T	J	D	U	A	O	R	N
N	R	O	A	U	D	J	T
R	N	A	O	D	U	T	J
J	T	U	D	O	A	N	R
U	D	J	T	N	R	O	A
A	O	R	N	T	J	D	U
O	A	N	R	J	T	U	D
D	U	T	J	R	N	A	O

Solution 97

8	6	3	1	7	5	4	2
7	5	4	2	8	6	3	1
6	8	1	3	5	7	2	4
5	7	2	4	6	8	1	3
4	2	7	5	3	1	8	6
3	1	8	6	4	2	7	5
2	4	5	7	1	3	6	8
1	3	6	8	2	4	5	7

i	h	g	f	e	d	c	b	a
c	b	a	i	h	g	f	e	d
f	e	d	c	b	a	i	h	g
h	g	i	e	d	f	b	a	c
b	a	c	h	g	i	e	d	f
e	d	f	b	a	c	h	g	i
g	i	h	d	f	e	a	c	b
a	c	b	g	i	h	d	f	e
d	f	e	a	c	b	g	i	h

H	J	L	K	I	N	O	M	P
M	P	O	J	L	H	I	N	K
N	K	I	P	O	M	L	H	J
P	O	M	L	H	J	N	K	I
K	I	N	O	M	P	H	J	L
J	L	H	I	N	K	M	P	O
I	N	K	M	P	O	J	L	H
L	H	J	N	K	I	P	O	M
O	M	P	H	J	L	K	I	N

n	l	j	h	f	d	b	o	m	k	i	g	e	c	a
m	k	i	g	e	c	a	n	l	j	h	f	d	b	o
l	j	h	f	d	b	o	m	k	i	g	e	c	a	n
k	i	g	e	c	a	n	l	j	h	f	d	b	o	m
j	h	f	d	b	o	m	k	i	g	e	c	a	n	l
i	g	e	c	a	n	l	j	h	f	d	b	o	m	k
h	f	d	b	o	m	k	i	g	e	c	a	n	l	j
g	e	c	a	n	l	j	h	f	d	b	o	m	k	i
f	d	b	o	m	k	i	g	e	c	a	n	l	j	h
e	c	a	n	l	j	h	f	d	b	o	m	k	i	g
d	b	o	m	k	i	g	e	c	a	n	l	j	h	f
c	a	n	l	j	h	f	d	b	o	m	k	i	g	e
b	o	m	k	i	g	e	c	a	n	l	j	h	f	d
a	n	l	j	h	f	d	b	o	m	k	i	g	e	c
o	m	k	i	g	e	c	a	n	l	j	h	f	d	b

Appendix 1

Diagonal Latin squares

For each order of square,
'a' and 'b' form an
orthogonal pair.

1	2	3	4	5
3	4	5	1	2
5	1	2	3	4
2	3	4	5	1
4	5	1	2	3

(a)

1	2	3	4	5
4	5	1	2	3
2	3	4	5	1
5	1	2	3	4
3	4	5	1	2

(b)

6	4	2	7	5	3	1
7	5	3	1	6	4	2
1	6	4	2	7	5	3
2	7	5	3	1	6	4
3	1	6	4	2	7	5
4	2	7	5	3	1	6
5	3	1	6	4	2	7

(a)

5	2	6	3	7	4	1
6	3	7	4	1	5	2
7	4	1	5	2	6	3
1	5	2	6	3	7	4
2	6	3	7	4	1	5
3	7	4	1	5	2	6
4	1	5	2	6	3	7

(b)

4	2	3	1
3	1	4	2
1	3	2	4
2	4	1	3

(a)

4	2	3	1
1	3	2	4
2	4	1	3
3	1	4	2

(b)

6	1	5	4	2	3
5	2	3	6	4	1
4	3	1	2	6	5
3	4	6	5	1	2
2	5	4	1	3	6
1	6	2	3	5	4

(single)

6	5	8	7	2	1	4	3
4	3	2	1	8	7	6	5
2	1	4	3	6	5	8	7
8	7	6	5	4	3	2	1
3	4	1	2	7	8	5	6
5	6	7	8	1	2	3	4
7	8	5	6	3	4	1	2
1	2	3	4	5	6	7	8

(a)

3	4	1	2	7	8	5	6
6	5	8	7	2	1	4	3
5	6	7	8	1	2	3	4
4	3	2	1	8	7	6	5
2	1	4	3	6	5	8	7
7	8	5	6	3	4	1	2
8	7	6	5	4	3	2	1
1	2	3	4	5	6	7	8

(b)

Appendix 2

Bibliography

Magic squares

There are few generally available titles that are entirely, or largely, about magic squares, although magic squares are a not uncommon feature of recreational mathematics.

Andrews, W. S., *Magic Squares and Cubes*, (Dover Publications). First published in 1917 from essays in an American journal (*The Monist*), this title seems always to be in print. Excellent basic reading.

Falkener, Edward, *Games Ancient and Oriental and How to Play Them*, (Dover Publications). Originally published in 1892, the book has a good section about magic squares. (In print, 1983).

Kraitchik, M., *Mathematical Recreations*, (Dover Publications). This title first appeared in 1942, and it has a great deal of useful magic square lore (In print, 1983).

Rouse Ball, W. W., *Mathematical Recreations and Essays*, (Macmillan). Originally published in 1892, this classic book has been out of print for several years, at least. Some public libraries still have copies. The book has a most valuable chapter devoted to magic squares (chapter enlarged at the eleventh (1939) edition).

Heath, Royal Vale, *Mathemagic*, (Dover Publications). Of the titles listed here, this one (which was first published in 1933) probably has most appeal for the semi-serious investigator of magic square matters. They form a small, but interesting, part of the whole (In print, 1983).

Latin squares

There seems to be but one currently available (and very substantial) title. It has been out of print for a few years, but a few institutions hold library copies that can be borrowed through the usual public library channels:

Dénes, J., and Keedwell, A. D., *Latin Squares and their Applications*, (English Universities Press, with others. A joint publicatioin in 1974). This is a serious academic contribution that, nevertheless, has parts to interest the highly numerate general reader.

I will also mention the following title which, although perhaps off-centre from our main themes, is not infrequently found upon the reference shelves of public libraries:

Fisher and Yates, *Statistical Tables*, (Oliver and Boyd). This standard work has something to say about Latin squares, and it has some pages of squares, ready made for the use of research workers (the intended readership).

Readers who develop an obsessive interest in magic squares will, I am sure, find further material to fuel their enthusiasm – including, possibly, titles that escaped my interested, but less than intensive, search.

About Latin squares; a more earnest search was needed to find even the single main title given above. Its extensive bibliography gives very many references, almost all of them of an academic nature.